Three words – life-changing, hilarious, inspiring.

A must read go to, dip in, easy to use, believe in and live by. A positive playful set of effervescence, energy, passion and drive detailed on every page which oozes the essence of Mary Rose's character. I laughed 'til I cried at the anecdotes witty insight and stories, and was left wanting more as to what happened next...

Alongside some fabulous stories the quizzes, moments of reflection, action points and simple applicable top tips, have made me stop pause and think, and have given me a platform to act with intention and purpose to do things differently for me, my life and business. I have begun my 'quest for my own harmony and expert status'.

This book will resonate with anyone who has had to juggle life, work, family, being a parent and being in business, and wants a helping hand to 'celebrate their life in harmony encompassing all that is important to them!' Like a guiding star, Mary Rose shows you the light...go on take it..... you are worth it!

Andi Lewis
Andi Lewis Consultancy

This book is a jewel, full of practical information, ideas and suggestions that will make essential reading for anyone building a home-based sales business. It will be at the top of my list for the women in my organisation. Great job Mary Rose, well done!

Yvonne Williams
Independent Senior National Sales Director, Mary Kay Cosmetics UK

It's a really brilliant resource, must have taken some time to put together! Lovely to have your stories woven into it. A very practical and thoughtful guide with mindset, spirit, and humour included.

Amanda Green
Emotional Health Coach

I really enjoyed it and think it has a lot of very interesting and hugely practical strategies for improving sales and being a professional sales person. Great job! I will be introducing this book to our team and am happy to promote it – well done for writing this. I am sure it will help and inspire many people over the years.

Heidi Blakeway
Director, The Fruitful Toolbox

Mary Rose is a marvel! Full of really practical and actionable advice, her straight-talking attitude especially appeals to me. I find her incredibly inspirational and very kind! I've seen how, when she talks to someone, she makes them believe in themselves, and then they start to shine! If you could bottle Mary Rose (and I think you should) you could sell it for millions.

Sam Ashdown
AshdownJones: The Lake District Estate Agents

Under the Sales Umbrella

Confidence boosting in sales: especially for women in small businesses selling products and services, including direct selling.

Mary Rose Selman

Published by Fossatello Group

Published by Fossatello Group

This edition first published 2019

by Fossatello Group, Yealand Conyers, Carnforth, Lancashire, LA5 9SN.

A catalogue record for this book is available from the Library of Congress

A catalogue record for this book is available from the British Library

ISBN: 978-1-9162743-0-3

Cover image by Katie Edwards.

Illustrations by Lou Simmonds.

Produced in Great Britain by York Publishing Services

www.yps-publishing.co.uk

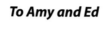

To Amy and Ed

It is just as honourable to sell
as it is to buy

Contents

Foreword

When I started my career in sales, telephones were attached to walls and the only 'tube' you were familiar with went on the inside of a bicycle tyre. You spoke to customers – now we 'connect' with them! Transactions happened with cash or personal cheque in real time and generally face to face. It was a different world. I had never sold anything in my life apart from when doing part-time jobs in school/ college holidays, and I can't recall selling anything other than a table-cloth even then. I didn't know if I would be any good at it, but I was coachable and I had a great product to sell.

Twenty-six years later I am still in awe of the product I continue to sell. I have learned my sales skills from the best and most generous group of people in sales who only wanted for my success. My job is to 'pass it on' – help other women to enjoy sales and selling, and to make whatever income they desire. Today I meet talented women who have great products or services but some are reluctant to sell because somehow being in sales has acquired a bit of a bad reputation. And yet shopping – going to buy something – *a sales transaction* – is almost a national past-time. Somewhere they have got their wires crossed!

I learned to sell products and I have had a profitable, satisfying and exciting career doing just that. I want every woman I meet to be able to tap into all the things I have learned, particularly those running small businesses and Sole Traders. I have worked alongside generous, talented, stylish, and wise women who have shared their expertise as I wish to do. I hope this book honours them. Here it is all written down in one place. There is nothing new and I am indebted to so many people over the years. I have aimed to acknowledge as many of them by name as I can recall!

I chose 'Under the Sales Umbrella' as a way of describing gathering all the useful information in one place, and heaven knows we all need a good umbrella! A good umbrella has at least 8 spokes and so the chapters fill that quota. Also, to lighten the mix, I have included some of my business anecdotes, which is where this book began.

MRS August 2019

Net Curtains and Olives

I have just pegged out my sparkling net curtains here in Italy. They will be seen by all my neighbours (it is a small village) and I feel a sense of satisfaction that I am demonstrating good housekeeping and organisation. My nets were grubby, that's the truth. In my defence, we don't live here all the time, and they were still full of the smoke and ash from Spring fires in the hearth, and so a job needing to be done. Net curtains are a necessity here to provide an element of privacy, as our house is on the road side, and it truly is a small village!

I live in two worlds: Lancashire and Umbria. My 'lives' couldn't be more different in each place, but both are wonderful; and for the present I do not want to change the status quo.

Lancashire is my English home. I am a wife, Mother and business woman running my cosmetics and sales training businesses from home. I am English. Umbria is my Italian home; there is no daily business to run there, but I am still a wife and Mother, and English.

In England my time is driven by the usual demands of family commitments, my work schedule and a few hobbies. In Italy my daily life is driven by what needs to be done: food, house and olive trees.

In both places my faith is fundamental to my life. In both places I live within walking distance of my churches, and they too are as different as chalk and cheese on the outside, but the same within.

A lot has been written about women and our work-life balance, reams of strategies about how to cope, self-help manuals, guidance and good practice, the list is endless. The implication being that you cannot exist in the present day as a working woman with a life (or vice versa) without a stress level that matches the national debt.

I disagree.

I think the phrase 'work-life balance' is too simplistic and provokes stress. It relies on an image of just two things that have to be equal to achieve balance. We know, as women, that just doesn't happen. Modern life is just not that tidy. There is always more going on.

I want to celebrate my life in harmony, encompassing all that is important to me: Faith, family, friends, home and work. I accept that harmony means all things coming together, "……a pleasing combination of elements in a whole……". It doesn't happen all the time, but it is the goal for which I strive.

As women we intuitively understand rhythms and cycles, whether we try to interfere with Mother Nature or not, we respond to life's challenges, daily, monthly or even seasonally. We are skilled at dealing with complexity and fearless when it comes to our responsibilities as mothers and carers. My life spans a time where combining faith, family, and a career, has gone from unusual to commonplace. We are living in age where we care for our children and our elderly parents whilst holding down a job at the same time.

Our role as women is evolving at great speed.

So, I think harmony is a better description of how we desire to live, weaving all the strands of our lives together. Focussing on what is important at the time, to create and preserve that harmony. Relishing when everything comes to that point be it a moment, a minute, a month, or a lifetime.

In Umbria my neighbours were baffled that I love to work in the olive grove whenever I am here – hot, cold, dry, wet, pruning or picking. Now they understand I do it because I love it. It has become a measured part of my life which brings contentment, joy, and the excitement of watching our Italian dream become a reality.

When I return to England, I love my world of cosmetics and sales and mentoring other women. It goes without saying that faith and family are my constants. Harmony is the ideal.

And washing the net curtains reminded me of all this. It may appear a simple task – it is, and yet very satisfying to complete. I'm guessing that my neighbours have nodded approval at my housekeeping skill. Was it life-changing? No. Was it life-affirming? Yes it was, because it was the most important thing to do today. And now done, I'll make a start on something else. Harmony...........

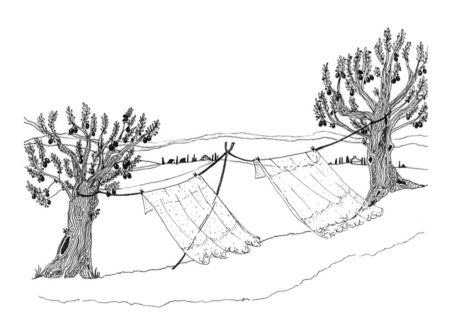

Introduction

Your Business Needs Sales!

"Nothing happens until somebody sells something"

This is one of the first 'sales quotes' I ever heard and it still has a simple power all these years later. Whether you are just starting out in business, have a product or a service to sell, or you have decided to accelerate your business to a new level, we need sales. Sales generate cash flow into your business. Sales are linked to profit and how you assess your business success.

Without sales income and profit we don't have a business, we have a hobby. Therefore sales should be exciting as they generate income. Most women enjoy going shopping. We like to buy, we don't like to be sold. Is this where the first round of sales antipathy springs from? The idea of some sales being about 'hard sell' and consequently sales people being 'pushy'. Do we dwell on cold calling telesales with mind-numbing scripts being followed and shop assistants with imposed sales targets to be met? Do we regard sales as being 'bold and brassy'?

I don't know, but somewhere along the line we seem to have become a bit conflicted and emotionally tangled up when it comes to sales! Or is it selling that gets the bad reputation? Are we all a bit sales cynical – 'caveat emptor' (meaning 'buyer beware') being the phrase that speaks in our head.

I'm going to lead you through my sales and selling skill sets and let you decide.

Our businesses need sales to survive and we probably need lots of sales to successfully grow our businesses. Let's ditch the old fashioned (dare I say masculine?) approach to sales with the hard edged phrases such as 'closing the sale', 'overcoming objections', and 'it's a numbers game' and enter the modern, female-inspired sales conversations that ensure our brand or our service generates sales and happy customers. Let's see if we can agree on ways to improve our sales by not concentrating on just a single transaction, but by aligning our product with our values and expertise, combined with exceptional customer service.

If you have a reluctant mindset when it comes to sales, let's see if we can create a personal checklist of simple sales skills that we can rely on and make good sales simple. What makes for a good sale? The obvious answer is a happy customer, but what about our side of the coin:

1.   A good product?

2.   A product that is competitively priced and presented?

3.   Good marketing to attract customers?

4.   Something 'different': what makes your product the chosen one?

The first three questions are easy to answer, the fourth may demand a little thought, but is really necessary to answer. In a world where the customer has product comparison at their fingertips instantly, what makes them decide to buy from you? And if the answer is 'me', that is perfectly fine too! In fact it's easier because you can work on yourself, your sales skill set, and productivity whenever you see fit. It is exactly what inspired me to name my sales training consultancy *Sell the Difference*, because so often we are the difference between a sale and the alternative!

Here are my suggestions for what leads to a good sale by simply making it a matter of choice:

1. 100% belief in your product or service.

2. Valuing yourself (confidence)

3. Having the ability to talk about your product.

4. Being the expert or 'go to' person in your market.

5. Having the ability to listen rather than tell.

6. Always delivering what you promise.

7. Developing a 'servant' mentality that builds customers for life.

8. Never forgetting that 'people buy from people'.

9. Learning how to accept rejection, expect it, and stop taking it personally.

10. Having fun.

We may passionately believe that we have a product that will, or does, sell itself, but the plain truth is that someone (you), has to get it in front of customers and help them make their choice. Someone does have to sell in the same way that someone has to buy to make the business work! Don't ignore it, get good at it, so that as a seller you have the satisfaction of knowing that your buyer, your customer, has what they wanted, needed or desired!

Over the next eight chapters I am going to give you some suggestions of how to do that to boost your confidence in the exciting world of sales and selling. I truly believe that building confidence builds better sales and profit, as well as enjoyment of running a profitable business.

Are you dating your business or is it a full-blown love affair?

For those of us following an entrepreneurial pathway, our business is very much a reflection of us and how we feel about it. Whether we are setting up as a sole trader within a larger company, a franchisee, or creator of a unique business, the beginning of our venture is the start of a journey of self-discovery. If you come from an employed background this is a new experience, and as with a new relationship forming, there are stages you will go through in just the same way as you fall in love (or out!). Of course there will always be some who fall head over heels in love, oblivious to problems, only having eyes for a blissful future, but most of us enter a new relationship with a little more caution. We are hopeful of happiness, but need more time before we commit.

"There's a difference between interest and commitment. When you're interested in doing something, you do it only when it's convenient. When you're committed to something, you accept no excuses – only results" Ken Blanchard.

I love that quote because it pretty much defines how I view setting up a new business and the efforts you make to ensure it is a success. I was a part-time entrepreneur for at least 12 months – just 'dating' my business because I had a full-time job that filled my days. My business was more of a project/hobby than a business. It was only when I developed a passion for it and wanted more from my part-time project, that I started to get serious about it. I was excited by the possibilities it was offering as a career choice. I needed to know more, sensing the gaps in my business skills and the practicalities of becoming a full blown, full-time entrepreneur. I wanted to spend more time with it, and it was beginning to fill up all my free time.

It was probably another 12 months of improving my business skills, studying more, investing in me more, before I realised that the courtship was completed. I was ready for commitment. There was no going back, the love affair was on! And that is when I left my employed job and followed my heart!

Patrick McGinnis talks about "The 10% Entrepreneur" and has written a book of the same name. I love that he positively encourages looking at entrepreneurship in a flexible way. It doesn't have to be all or nothing, even if it ends up that way. My experience of part-time entrepreneurship for quite a long period of time, was happy and productive in just the way I wanted. It gave me a safe 'taster time' which is really important for women. I was happy with dating my business. 10% can be good – it can be exactly what you want. And as with love affairs, a high proportion of start-ups don't necessarily work out. But when they do, the results are life-changing.

How do you feel about your business? Are you happy with the relationship or do you want more? A lot is written about goal setting and achievement. However, I think you have to have a vision of where you want the relationship with your business to go, and if you are ready and willing to take things to the next level. My vision took me from part-time to 100% entrepreneur, and my first business celebrates its 26th Anniversary this year!

Chapter 1

Image and Confidence

> **"Self-confidence is the foundation of all great success and achievement"**
> *Brian Tracy*

If you are running a business, sales and selling are your 'bread and butter', your cash flow and an indicator of success. If it is your own business, then you take responsibility for sales as much as for any other part of your organisation. If you are working as part of, or running, a sales team, you will have clear guidelines and sales targets that need to be achieved. There is an added layer of accountability.

If the world is ready and waiting to buy your product or service, are you ready to sell? Are you equipped for success? Have you got 100% belief in your product? And my last question, are you confident about you and the image you project? (The same would go for a sales team for which you are responsible or lead.)

I have yet to meet a woman who successfully sells a product which she doubts in some way. For a product to come to market there have to be a variety of things coming together to make the final package. Women feel more confident when everything is in harmony: product, packaging, price, value, worth, availability, customer service post-purchase, to name but a few. We like to know about what we sell. We may have invested financially in our product or service, which adds to the emotional investment we make when we start to sell it. Our confidence level increases when we are "sure" about our product or service. The 100% belief is matched by an enthusiasm it produces and the two together provide the perfect foundation for selling to potential customers.

It matters how the product is presented or packaged, it must attract and be attractive for a sale to be possible. It also matters how the person handling the sale presents themselves in the marketplace as they represent the brand or are delivering the service. What you look like does have an impact on the outcome of the sale. Do not underestimate the speed with which a judgement call is made about you at the same time as your product. Your image is important. Image and confidence go together. When you feel relaxed about the former, because you have given it some thought, you become the best walking business card for your product or service. Think of why uniforms were invented or why some companies require dress codes. They want their brand to be recognised and to have a certain style – an unspoken standard reflecting how they see themselves and how they want to be seen. Their employees' image is defined.

When we work for ourselves, surely we should spend some time considering our image? How confident are you that you 'look the part' and represent the brand? This isn't vanity, this is part of the sales process and is worth attention! Working in the cosmetics industry, representing a top brand, meant that I had to learn how to apply make up to a professional standard using the products that I sold. I wanted to be authentic and it was important to me. The learning process certainly helped me acquire product knowledge too!

Are you confident about your image? It may not be that you can use your product in the same way that I describe, but as women in sales it is important to us that we are authentic as well as being 100% one hundred percent behind our product or service. Checking that we have a professional appearance when we are going to work with customers shows that we care. Does the outer you reflect the inner you? A quick way to check is to take a selfie right now and see if you are happy with the picture. Are you happy with your image? Is this how you present yourself to customers? If you really don't like what you see, it's probably time to do something about it. I'm not talking surgery, just a little extra attention!

> **"Be yourself, everyone else is already taken"**
> *Oscar Wilde.*

First impressions do matter. In our fast-paced world it is now recognised that seven seconds is all the time you have to make a first impression. It is barely time to smile and say your name, so it is worth reviewing your appearance. It may sound flippant, but it's probable that however lovely you are, however exceptional your product, or empowering your service, if you turn up at a professional business meeting or networking session, or any selling appointment looking less than smart, professional and 'put together', you may spend an inordinate amount of time correcting the wrong first impression of you and your product. The knack is to always look appropriate. You reflect your business so dress accordingly.

Here is my check-list top-to-toe whatever your product or service!

1.   Have your hair professionally cut regularly.

2.   Wear make-up – appropriately – don't panic, lipstick and mascara count,

3.   Notice when you receive compliments about your choice of clothes. Wear those styles and colours more often.

4.   Armpits are never appealing – choose sleeves!

5.   A wise Sales Trainer and Mentor friend called Carolyn O'Neill said to me – 'The eye is drawn where the line ends'. Consider this when it comes to skirt length and cleavage. I leave you to

contemplate that…! Let's not have confusion about exactly what we are selling.

6.   Uniforms are no excuse to hide behind. If it is hideous smile more! If it's Prada – lucky you!

7.   In a casual age it is all right to stand out from the crowd with a defined 'smart look'. It may turn out to be a really good thing if it makes you and your product memorable.

8.   If it is more appropriate to be casual, apply all of the above but, ladies, rarely does Lycra sell outside a gym!

And if you still feel uneasy about your image, why not get some professional help? Your local women's networking groups probably have wonderful image consultants offering a service to help you develop your own style.

*Find a **balance** so that your image becomes*
an innate awareness of self.

While we are reviewing our outer image, how do we feel about inner self and confidence levels? Do you have an inner voice that acts as a critic? And does your inner voice determine your actions and confidence? As women we recognise that we all have such a voice. I once read it described as Risk Aversion meets Health and Safety. Good for stopping us jumping off very high buildings, not so good if it stops us from being successful sales people with a constant drip of doubt that saps our confidence. If you don't already know it, let me introduce you to the female 80:20 rule. It's the one that makes us dwell on the 20% of what we can't do, don't have etc, rather than the 80% of our brilliance. Our inner voice is masterful at this especially as we change our outer image or learn the new skills of sales and selling. It may run something like this:-

'What do you think you look like'?

'What made me think I could wear ......?' (insert new stylish item of clothing).

'What makes you think you can learn how to do this?'

'This is not for you, sales people are pushy and loud'.

For all thoughts that begin: 'You're not ......' and end '.........enough', insert words like clever, pretty, knowledgeable, good, thin, confident etc. If you listen to it, that inner voice can paralyse you and remove all your confidence in a few words. Consider this: making changes, or learning a new skill, is to step out of your comfort zone and into the unknown; that is when the inner voice is loudest (remember Risk Aversion!). The habit to develop is to hear it, but not listen. Realistically it carries no value in this situation. Why let it determine your choices? Turn down the volume of the voice, don't have an argument with it as you'll never win – just create delay and denial.

Quiet the voice of criticism and liberate more positive confident you! (See book suggestion in Resources, Further Reading and Inspiration: *Playing Big* by Tara Mohr).

You can develop greater self-confidence by replacing the negative doubts with a few daily mindset motivational switches. Try these:

- Start the day by reading something positive preferably before your feet touch the floor!

- Pay yourself a few compliments

- Pat yourself on the back for new accomplishments.

- Don't bat away compliments with self-conscious denial, learn to say "thank you" and smile.

- Celebrate your successes (however small) along the way.

Working on your confidence level is not an indulgence or self-absorption, it's a useful starting point to get to know and accept things about yourself and particularly how you approach sales and selling. There is no doubt that confidence matched with enthusiasm helps you sell more. Having had a review of our image, the next step is to think about how our personality impacts our sales and selling style, particularly when dealing with prospective customers.

You may have completed a workplace behavioural profile as an employee; many companies used them as part of an interview process or leadership development programme. DiSC® is my preferred diagnostic method in my sales and selling "vocabulary". Working with the DiSC® behaviour assessment techniques has helped me discover things about myself and how I respond to people and they to me. DiSC® has helped me identify and work to my strengths. It is low key, engaging, easy to pick up and retain as a "sales tool".

Look at the following and judge how you respond – mark them in importance from 1-4:

You are a results person

You exude enthusiasm and love a challenge

Accuracy is important to you

Being secure and having a strong support system is how you function best

There is no right or wrong answer. We identify with one or maybe two of those statements. The statements are simplistic examples of the DiSC® system based on four different personality types:

Dominance – the results person

Influence – the enthusiastic action person

Conscientiousness – the accurate person

Steadiness – the secure dependable person

Which style is most like you?

Quick quiz!

1.   Which word sums you up?

a)   Patient

b)   Persuasive

c)   Decisive

d)   Fact-finder

2. Do you:

a)   Work at a steady pace

b)   Like to get things done quickly

c)   Focus on the big picture

d)   Focus on details

3. For your holidays, do you:

a)   Make sure everyone is happy with the choice before you book

b)   Pack your bag and grab a flight to the sunshine

c)   Decide the destination in advance based on fact finding and good reviews

d)   Plan in detail and pack meticulously

Results!

If you chose answers that were mostly c, then your style tends towards Dominance.

If you chose answers that were mostly b, then your style tends towards Influence.

If you chose answers that were mostly a, then your style tends towards Steadiness.

If you chose answers that were mostly d, then your style tends towards Conscientiousness.

Our DiSC® profile is part of our behavioural image. We can adapt our behaviour to improve our business performance, just as we can alter our image. We can recognise other people's profiles and style which gives us a confidence in how we interact them. How we start that 'sales conversation', how we make a customer connection. By asking the right questions, observing the way our customers speak and act, helps us find 'common ground' for a satisfactory sale. There is more about DiSC® profiling in Chapter 5.

Image and confidence go together. The reassuring fact is that just as you can alter your image, you can improve your self-confidence. Do confident people sell more? I would say yes, if applied to authentic confidence which comes from 100% belief and knowledge as mentioned at the beginning of this chapter. Lack of confidence leads towards uncertainty and doubt which transmits to the potential customer or client, which in turn diminishes the chance or choice of purchase.

And lastly confidence doesn't mean loud and noisy. Sometimes the noisy outgoing people are using it as a smokescreen to cover nerves and a lack of confidence. Do you know that quiet people make the best sales people because they take more time to listen to their customers?

> *"God didn't have time to make a nobody, just a somebody. You are somebody. Self-confidence is there if you will just dig deep enough to find it. It can propel you into the position to become the person God meant you to be"*
>
> *Mary Kay Ash*

Goal Setter or Dreamweaver?

Are you one, the other or both?

When I started my business I knew that I had to have goals. Primarily it was to replace my employed income (crucial to family life) and to have more flexibility of time (equally crucial to family life). I subscribed totally to S.M.A.R.T. goals (Specific, Measurable, Achievable, Relevant, Time-bound) as described in all business training manuals. In fact I found it quite reassuring to write it all down. It gave my embryo business a gravitas and direction.

But it didn't make my pulse race.

It wasn't until I attended a Business Retreat in Manchester Massachussetts, led by my friend and mentor Anne Newbury, that I discovered why. Over 48 hours I was immersed in the company of successful women who were dream-inspired as well as goal setters. I found there is a difference and most importantly that I was, and am, a Dreamer!

For me goals are the plans that can be externally measured and monitored. Dreams are entirely personal. The timescale is unique to you; they are the things that drive you out of bed and into action on what might otherwise be a duvet day. Dreams are the things that you allow yourself to imagine might one day be possible. And goals help that dream have a step by step progression from dream to reality. My dreams made my pulse race. They gave my business a personal purpose. They made me want to set goals and achieve them. They gave me a 'Why'.

Dream-inspired goal setting was instantly more appealing than S.M.A.R.T. Here is what has become a business foundation, with grateful thanks to that remarkable group of women back in 1996.

I like the mantra – I like the resonance of the 'Ds' in the Dream-inspired goal setting below. I like that they can bring a sharpness and definition to my dreams. I like the challenge to be daring!

Dream-inspired goal setting:

- *DECIDE and DEFINE: Decide what your goals are, define them and write them down in **BOLD PRINT** (it means you mean it). Be clear. Be simple.*

- *DECLARE: Declare your goals to someone you respect. Make copies of your goals and post them everywhere obvious, to remind yourself daily.*

- *DEDICATE: Invest in yourself, dedicate some time to learning and honing the skills you will need to achieve these new goals.*

- *DEFEND: Be prepared to defend your decisions. There are always people ready to 'rain on your parade'. Know your 'Why'.*

- *DELEGATE: try getting help for tasks that stop you from achieving your goal.*

- *DELIVER: Commit 100% to what you have planned. Make daily affirmations to reinforce your commitment, say them OUT LOUD!*

- *DISCIPLINE: Imperative! Mary Kay Ash told us that "Working will, where wishing won't"! You have great products and services, introduce them to new people every day. It takes discipline to build a successful business (applicable to any product/service).*

- *DARE: To believe that you can do more than you think!*

Chapter 2

Mindset Matters

> **"Your attitude determines your altitude"**
> *Zig Zigler*

From knowing nothing about sales to becoming an 'expert' in my own field, has been an adventure. Making the change from employed to self-employed and building a business was a huge leap of faith. *'Your attitude determines your altitude'* is the popular phrase inspired by Zig Zigler.

It is undeniable that a positive mental attitude has a huge impact, not only on our confidence levels but on our ability to bounce back from life's challenges. Do not underestimate the need to spend time doing *'a check-up from the neck up'* daily (more words from Zig Zigler). I love this quote. to me it means working on the inner mindset as well as the outer image that everyone sees.

The outer image is pretty simple to work on. The inner you is much more complex, especially in a world where women still juggle many responsibilities: home, work, family, life and death and the bit in between. We feel busier than ever, bombarded by a continuous stream of 'noise' and probably less content and judged more (and found wanting).

How many of these sound familiar:

–   I'm always on the go

–   My to-do list is never done

–   I am constantly tired

–   My time is not my own

–   What "Me" time? Life's a blur

–   I feel overwhelmed

–   What made me think I could start a business?

These feelings do not encourage a positive attitude. I'm not suggesting you ignore them, but if we are to develop a positive attitude we have to address them. No one buys from a miserable sales person. Sales are not fun if you are feeling drab. Worry is not a good look. What helped me establish an optimism alongside developing a positive attitude was understanding what was going on as both a new entrepreneur and new sales person. There are is a difference between selling for someone else and selling for yourself, but there are also a few common points.

Here's a list of thoughts that have helped me along the way. Agree and add your own thoughts, or disagree and cross some out, but take a few moments to think about how you can develop and maintain a positive attitude in sales. We need Bounce-back-ability! We need a sense of humour! We need a vision and a plan. We need to find opportunities to celebrate small victories!

> **"Head, Heart, and Soul – search for harmony rather than balance!"**
> *Mary Rose Selman*

1. Finding my 'why'. Why was I starting in sales and what was my purpose in setting up sales business?

    If you have created your product or are overwhelmingly wedded to the benefits of your service, this might appear easy to answer. If you started your business as an alternative to something else, it will need a little more consideration. In either case it is fundamental and must be answered. Give your 'Why' a voice. Speak it out loud.

2. Learning not to lose sight of that purpose or being distracted away from it.

    It almost seems as though the gods and the universe conspire against you when you embark on a new venture! You name it and it will happen. Having a clear purpose enables you to keep afloat like Noah's Ark, when all around you seems to be chaos. It helps to have a sturdy vessel. A purpose that keeps you buoyant!

3. Allowing time to move away from an employed mentality towards an entrepreneurial one.

    Learning to make my own business decisions and choices! It wasn't instantaneous for me, or easy. On reflection, this becomes a really important point. In an age of instant success/ gratification/supply/demand it is all too easy to be swept up in self-doubt. Allowing yourself time to work *on* your business as well as *in* your business, will bear fruit. Knowing that there will be self-doubt diminishes its destructive impact.

4. Becoming an eternal student interested in knowing more about my business and constantly developing my skill set.

    I write about being the expert in this book, which is the obvious learning curve of developing a service or working with a product. Expanding a business or leading a sales team as the

22

leader requires that you learn more about business techniques that will benefit others.

Although not directly associated with sales, being fascinated by selling has broadened my horizons and my business. I give myself permission to explore and expand my knowledge. I invest in myself through learning.

5. Loving my business, but learning to make business decisions with my head, as well my heart, being true to my purpose.

    Always a tricky one for us women, we get emotional. I have the most supportive, interested, wise husband, but I needed a female business mentor to help me find my way around this one. I wish the same for you. Find someone you respect and preferably is 'where you would like to be'. Ask for mentoring help. Women love to help other women.

6. Deciding not to give up easily but learning to pause, regroup, learn from mistakes without emotion.

    I have always taken my business seriously.

7. Understanding that on average 50% of people will choose to buy from someone else. Get over it. Get in front of more people!

    You have to work on handling the feeling of rejection when people do not buy from you. Understanding it is their choice, not taking it personally, moving on to the next sales opportunity. And not giving up, but assessing why it didn't go your way this time. It doesn't leave you, but you do get faster at dealing with it by developing a sense of proportion, and longer-term thinking.

> ***"Stop thinking things that people think,***
> ***that they don't think at all!"***
> *Anne Newbury*

8. Setting a weekly sales target from Day 1 of my business was a considered action. I knew what my business had to produce in sales to pay the business bills and provide profit for running our home. Not enough people equated to not enough sales, based on the selling to 50% average.

9. Women buy on emotion and justify with logic (except for shoes……).

    It was a mindset to learn to make sure that I provided great customer service in order to ensure my customers stayed with me, re-ordered, and referred their friends. After the excitement of purchase (for both of us!) comes an important building of a customer relationship.

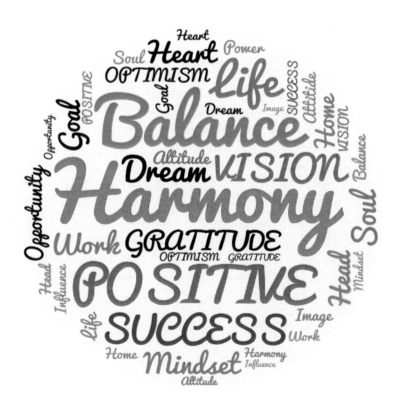

10. Being flexible – customers are people first.

    This meant setting up systems that suited my customers so that they could contact me when necessary, re-order products when it suited them, finding solutions to problems, not panicking and taking a problem as a criticism. Be prepared to go the extra mile to make them feel valued (which they are!).

11. Expecting abundance and celebrating small victories. (And sometimes small sales!).

    When you set a weekly sales target and meet or exceed it, celebrate! Create a habit of celebration even if it a cup of coffee and slice of cake!

12. Being grateful. Finding gratitude *every day*, even when it takes a while!

    Start a daily gratitude journal or find a gratitude buddy to exchange experiences with.

13. Getting help before getting desperate! (Either in the business or in the home). <u>For most women I think this is key</u>.

    I thought I was Superwoman. I was not. There is a saying you must 'Give up to go up'. I took that to mean that in order to put my best efforts into my sales business, I need to give up something that I could delegate. I have learned that 'Giving up' on certain tasks has been fundamental to growing a successful business. From getting domestic help in my home, through to office help in my business, to choosing a great accountant.

    All of that type of help frees me to be more productive in my business, not to mention being more organised and calm outside it.

14. Noting that I do have the ability to think about my business all the time, but I do not <u>need</u> to do it all the time!

15. Your family will always love you as you love them. Include them from the start.

    Our children were young when I started my business. They did not understand my career change, but they did know I was now working from home. They helped me define my business in practical terms: for example hours, time management, planning, and together we planned 'treats' that my business would provide as it grew (early goal setting!).

    They defined my purpose: that my family's well-being was fundamental to my business choices. All too often we feel guilt as working mothers, but including your children in why you are working explaining as you go along has certainly eased my level of guilt, but there is always a niggle of doubt!

16. Develop a sense of urgency: setting goals, making decisions, looking for opportunities.

    As my friend and colleague Bella O'Hara says "Make your intentions clear, don't let them slip away. Imagine yourself in that position as though you've already done it".

    As Paul McCartney sings: "Do it now while your vision is clear......." (*Do It Now*, Paul McCartney, Egypt Station, 2018, Capitol Records).

"One of the things I learned the hard way was that it doesn't pay to get discouraged. Keeping busy and making optimism a way of life can restore your faith in yourself."

Lucille Ball

Having a Business Baby

It occurs to me that starting a new business, or taking on a new business, is a bit like having a baby and then raising your baby to adulthood.

It starts as such a great idea and even a plan!

Creating a baby is one thing ….

Imagining yourself as a Yummy Mummy with a perfectly adorable baby and a happy balanced life, is another thing….

Fantastic!

But the bit you didn't quite register, didn't quite factor in, or maybe just blissfully ignored, is the day to day reality of living with this precious little being and then becoming responsible for every outcome that affects them for years and years and years!

I think you 'get' where I am going with this analogy, so let's just insert 'business' for 'baby' and keep going.

One more thing before that, here is my list of three top truths:

1. All babies are different.

2. You love your baby more than anyone else's baby.

3. You find you would do literally anything to make sure your baby develops healthily, happily and surrounded by love.

OK back to starting a business. Linking in to my Top Truths, if you feel that way at the outset of starting your business, you do indeed have your Business Baby. And babies and businesses need attention on a regular basis. In the very early days minute by minute as you get used to each other and find a routine.

The joy of creating is overwhelmingly matched by the awesome responsibility that you have taken on.

It's tiring. You knew it would be, but you never envisaged the level of tiredness you now see as part of your daily life.

Good practical advice is oh so welcome in this uncharted territory. However sometimes there is just too much of it to decide which is good, not so good, or even applies to you! Meeting other people at the same stage as you is a delight. You have an instant peer group support system of shared experiences.

You find there are so many things you never knew you needed before your Business Baby arrived! All of them appear crucial. And even the niggling thought that perhaps this was not such a good idea…….. but it's too late now.

I have good news for you if you stick it out, ask any successful business owner how they feel about creating/setting up and running a business, or being self-employed and generally you will find that they are immensely proud of what they have achieved. That the 'return on investment' was worth every extra hour spent nurturing the growth and development of their business.

Had they challenges and setbacks? Of course! Sleepless nights wondering what on earth they had done? Most certainly! Found out things about themselves and learned new skills and talents? Without doubt! And the most interesting question for me, would they do it all over again? Was it worth it? With a wry smile most, if not all, say "Of course, in a heartbeat!"

Chapter 3

Memorable Me

> **"The three fastest means of communication:
> telephone, telegraph, tell-a-woman"**
> *Susanna Pomeroy, 1956.*

I first heard this 'saying' 20 years ago! Pre-social media, pre-Google, and I'm not sure everyone knows what 'telegraph' means these days! I am sure that word of mouth is still valid and a powerful way to communicate the merits of your product, and word of mouth referrals always bring great sales. You have a great product or service and you are happy with its production and presentation, now is time to start letting the world know about it. Communication and how you go about it is the emphasis of this chapter.

The simple truth is that the more people are introduced to your product the greater opportunity for sales. In that sense it is a 'numbers game'. Marketing attracts and drives potential customers to your product and if done effectively, the most interested in purchasing will want to connect with you. Even in a world where on-line marketing and social media marketing are hyped as most important, I am still totally interested in your personal performance. Not only do you have to understand how your marketing works, you have to be able to add your personal touch to it and pick up the sale where the marketing ends.

I am interested in the sale, the transaction, but well aware that it doesn't happen in isolation. You do need to be cognisant of the marketing attached to building your brand. If you are running your own business it is your choice whether you outsource and employ marketing professionals or do it yourself. Social media does give huge opportunity to small business owners to get to grips with the basics of marketing themselves. (I refer to the obvious platforms of Facebook, LinkedIn, Twitter, Pinterest, and Instagram in Chapter 7). Whether you have a superlative support team marketing for you, or you are on your own, I am sure you still understand the value and love to get out there into the field and make sure you and your business or brand are memorable for all the right reasons, making the drive from marketing to successful sales transactions seamless.

In a crowded marketplace (unless you have created something unique) you have to have something that makes you different from the rest when it comes to attracting that purchasing customer. There is generally a point when customers want to connect with you, be it for information, clarification or reassurance. You make a difference in the space between marketing and the sale. You could be the deciding factor between a 'maybe' and a 'yes'!

Are you ready and prepared to meet the purchasing public and speak? (Out of the numbers the sales will come).

If you represent your brand you will talk about it a lot. The sales process starts from introducing yourself to your potential client/customer. Remember those 7 seconds to make a first impression. By the time you've started to speak we know your outer image has been observed, and opinion formed!

It is worth practising how and what you are going to say in that brief window of time.

Here are my suggestions. Choose and put together what suits your style and lasts 7 seconds:

1. Smile (not grin) – it's the shortest distance between two people (*Viktor Borge*).

2. Say your name – a name badge is always useful; wear it on the right side at shoulder height which is much easier for your customer to see and read.

3. Add a brief description – e.g. I represent…..working with….. as….. your job title…..creator of….

4. Offer a handshake – outstretched hand waist high; simple clasp don't pump up and down.

5. Offer a business card – have your picture on it; people will remember your face long after they've forgotten your name.

6. Ask for their name if appropriate.

7. Allow 'space' for them to answer!

8. Be ready with the next question to start the conversation – e.g. How can I help you? Have you heard of us? Is there a question that I can answer? Would you like more details? Even a comment about the weather is fine if it seems to put the person at ease. (Rumour has it that HM The Queen favours "Have you come far?" to fill any awkward gap when meeting people!)

7 seconds – make them count!

To reach more people the quickest way is to personally do some Business Networking. It also has the bonus of helping you make new business friends, collect referrals and you will raise your profile and that of your product, whilst building your confidence. There are business networks everywhere, they are easy to find through the internet and worth the price of a cup of coffee to investigate. You will find the ones that suit you and your product, don't waste any time on the ones that don't work for you. You will need your business cards and to be able to introduce yourself and your business as suggested. In addition, you will be asked to introduce yourself to the group and be given a minute or two to do it.

Do not panic! It is normal to feel nervous when you first do it. What I want to suggest is that you have a 'wardrobe' of introductions ready to "choose and use' in much the same way as you selected for your 7 seconds. I suggest thinking about and planning for 3 situations where an introduction is needed. They are defined by the length of time you have to speak at the event and whether or not you are introducing yourself or being introduced.

This basic 60 second introduction works well for any networking situation, followed by how to speak about your business for longer periods of time:

A 60 second basic introduction
(and have a prop such as a brochure, product, business card).

An introduction followed by a 10 minute talk about your business
(have a prop and use prompt cards).

An introduction followed by a 20 minute talk about your businesss
(use prompt cards to help you stay on track and on time).

So, what do I say?

The really important thing to do is start with your name and business, and repeat it again at the end. You want people to be able to do any, or all of the following:

1. Find your website after the meeting

2. To like your Facebook page

3. Join your club

4. Follow you on Instagram/Twitter/Pinterest

5. Buy your product

6. Recommend you to someone else.

7. Connect with you on LinkedIn

The 60 second introduction

Fill in the blank spaces with your information. Introduce yourself by name.

1. Your full name

2. Your business full name

3. What is your business about

    (the less words the better, be succinct!)

4. Where you work from – home/office/shop

5. Why you started or got involved with your business

    (women are really interested in this)

6. What you love about your business

    (gives your product/service a unique personality)

7. Example/brochure/invitation to visit, or what you're looking for as a result of the meeting

8. Repeat your name and business

This is probably the most important introduction you will create, because it is the one you will use most at the beginning of any speaking in public. It is also useful if you have to 'Go Fishing'! (see chapter 7).

Introduction followed by the 10 Minute Talk

You may have a choice of introducing yourself, or someone else does it for you. So write your 60 second introduction ready for either situation. Your talk should be a brief resume of you and your business life to date. You could also choose to include:

- your accolades, those things that are identifiable and of which you are proud. eg Business Awards

- Your professional qualifications and any publications.

- A little about your family if that is appropriate.

- Something personal like a hobby, or what you like to do in your spare time.

- Your achievements or something of which you are proud since starting your business

- Your future plans

In other words, flesh out the 60 second introduction, and tell your story.

The Introduction followed by 20 Minute Presentation

This is likely to be in the situation where you are being introduced, using the written introduction you have prepared yourself. In addition to the previous examples you may want to create a product display, so check availability of a display table and area at the venue. A PowerPoint presentation might be useful to consider as you have more time. Simple visuals are received best rather than detailed written information.

Be careful of using humour unless you know your audience well. Allow time for a brief question and answer situation; don't fret about being unable to answer a question – but do make sure that you can source the answer and get back to the person later. You will definitely need prompt cards and they help steady the nerves by existing!

Suggestions for planning:

1. Thank you to whoever has introduced you, and re-state why you've been asked to speak.

2. More about you and your business, to add colour and individuality.

3. Engage the audience with questions – eg Have they tried? Have they used? Do they have a favourite brand?

4. Presentation of your product or service in more detail (e.g. display or Powerpoint or sampling).

5. Tell stories about your business – use some humour if appropriate.

6. Share plans for your business.

7. Invitation with a special offer – including reminder of product display and information.

8. Re-state your accessibility via your web site and social media.

9. Available right now for a further chat.

It's all about You! Once written, practise them out loud to build your confidence. Remember the audience has already used up 7 seconds forming a first impression of you. Lucky we got the image bit sorted out early on because now is your VIP moment – and remembering to breathe. Controlling your voice helps to control your nerves!

VIP = Volume, Intonation, and Pitch

Volume: depends on the size of the room, but rarely do you need to talk at much louder than normal. If you judge the room to be so large it will swallow the sound, then speak up – you have a message to deliver. If the room is full of people that will absorb sound, use a little extra volume.

Intonation: before you speak, smile and breathe, it will give you a moment to relax. Ideally think of an arc for each sentence that will give a flow and a rhythm. Pausing is good. Practice simply saying your full name and the full name of your business in one breath.

Pitch: the smile and breathe routine really works when it comes to pitch. Nerves tend to make us seize up and that can send our voice up an octave, and then we are distracted by a voice that doesn't sound like us at all. We speed up to get it over. Clarity, is the word on which to focus. You know your name and business and everyone in the room is interested to hear it too.

Slow and steady wins the race!

The skill of speaking in public is to get your message across simply and clearly. Concentrate on the message, and who you are trying to connect with, not yourself. That's why it is worth having your introductions prepared. Remember image, appearance and first impression are over by the time you say 'Hello', it's what you SAY next that is important. I encourage you to stand to speak. It demonstrates confidence. It gets everyone's attention. It gives you time to take that important breath. You can see all the people you are talking to. Smile (not grin). Make eye contact, look around the group, then greet them.

Please, please, *please*, don't stand up and say you're nervous – it transmits that feeling to your audience and now they are worried too!

If you have decided that to be memorable your presentation will involve technology, make sure you arrive well in advance of your allotted time to make sure the equipment is functioning and that you can work it yourself. Always have a back-up plan in case of power/ equipment failure.

The ABC checklist of communicating effectively.

As

Audience: who and how many?

Accolades: they add emphasis and colour.

Appropriate: image and authenticity

Bs

Bright: decide to enjoy the moment.

Build: decide what you want as the result from the talk.

Business like: choose your words to convey the right message.

Cs

Clear: name, business, opportunity

Confident: prepared (props and prompts are just fine).

Concise: remember VIP, no dithering allowed.

And finally, choose your words! Some of them can be really irritating to the listener!

BANISH AND BIN	KEEP AND ADD
So *(at the start of every sentence)*	Excited to
Sorry *(each time you pause)*	Personal attention
Err	Simple
Um	Tried and Tested
A little bit *(preceding any form of anxiety)*	Customer service
Just	Integrity
Actually	Opportunity
Almost	Free
Does that make sense? *(only if you've made it confusing)*	Special offer
Off the top of my head *(why don't you know?)*	Affordable
Like	Step by step
Cheap	Inexpensive

One last thing!

> *"The right word may be effective, but no word was ever as effective as a rightly timed pause"*
> *Mark Twain*

You know you've gained self-confidence when you can learn to insert and time a pause when you are speaking!

A simple smile could lead
to a million special things

For my High School Yearbook (1971) quote, I chose:

"A smile is the shortest distance between two people!"
Viktor Borge

I had just completed a year in the USA attending and graduating High School in Massachussetts. I lived with a wonderful family for my year away. These days it sounds much like any other 'gap' type experience, but back then I left my family and friends and saw them 12 months later. Communication was by post and we had to book international telephone calls. I spoke to my parents twice: Christmas Day and my 18th Birthday.

For a year I had made friends, experienced a new school system and more than that, had been absorbed by a completely different culture. Smiling and saying: "Hello" happened a lot. Thrown in at the deep end as I stepped off the plane at Boston, it was sink or swim: make friends or don't. Smiling, saying "Hello" and introducing myself became second nature.

I also made a decision to say yes to all sorts of adventures and experiences that opened my world and expanded my horizons. I learned to sail and discovered the beauty of the coastline from Cape Cod to Maine. I learned to ski and discovered that I was never going to choose skiing as a recreational sport again after that winter! I joined a modern dance group and fell in love with the Martha Graham technique, which did change my life direction. And I spent a month working for a Congressman as an Intern in Washington DC…..Chappaquidick, Astronauts, Purple Hearts, White House, Congress and Senate were all part of those 30 days!

And truthfully all of those experiences which shaped my life, came from making a decision to join in, smile and say "Hello" to new people and new challenges.

Without realising it, I was developing what we now call a Positive Attitude! Constantly meeting new people can be exhausting and overwhelming, so those that return smiles become the ones you choose to get to know. And smiling is scientifically proven to make you feel better, happier, less stressed, more attractive, and apparently can even lower your heart rate and blood pressure. Combine that with being able to say "Hello" and your name, and you have an instant recipe for success.

Mother Teresa said: "Every time you smile at someone, it is an action of love, a gift to that person, a beautiful thing!"

After 25 years of running a successful business as a Mary Kay Consultant and Director, I am often asked for practical tips on how I got started. I believe I was fortunate to be given great advice by my Mary Kay mentors, that I have always tried to pass on and much of it depends on simply adding a smile!

The 3 foot rule – be ready to smile and introduce yourself and your business to anyone who comes within that distance. (And if appropriate, offer them the opportunity to try your product).

Communicating by phone – 'Smile before you dial' and if you can't or won't – don't! Nowadays the same principle applies to all forms of communication.

'Pretend that every single person you meet has a sign around his or her neck that says: Make me feel important.' (after Mary Kay Ash).

Never forget this message when working with people. Learn to look for and pay them sincere compliments with a smile. If Mary Kay Ash asked you how you were, she expected the answer "I'm Great" said with a smile. Your brain works on what you feed it. Smile and be positive.

So, a simple smile can lead to a million special things. Isn't that exciting and tantalizing?

Chapter 4

Conversational Sales

"Practice is just as valuable as a sale. The sale will make you a living; the skill will make you a fortune"
Jim Rohn

What is Conversational Sales? Simply put, it is a dialogue-driven approach to sales whereby a relationship is developed with a potential customer that allows them to be the central focus of any transaction. The sale occurs after the customer's desires, needs, questions are met and answered and they are ready to purchase. There are no scripts to follow. There is no sales patter. There is a genuine interest in making sure the customer gets what they want. I believe this suits us as women in sales because we like to develop high trust sales built on relationships. And we have those three attributes of: Intuition, Listening and Nurturing,

*We are **intuitive** – we are good at 'reading between the lines'*
*We are good **listeners** – therefore we ask questions*
*We are **nurturers** – customer experience and service are paramount.*

All of these help us succeed at this type of selling.

Are you coachable? I knew I needed to learn how to sell Mary Kay skincare products if my business plan was to work! The good news is that selling is a skill and skills can be taught. Learning a new skill means allowing time to practise until your confidence grows. If you are just starting out in sales remember to give yourself some time.

Enthusiasm sells, being a practiced professional sells more! You are ready. Your product is ready. You are happy with your marketing. You've started telling the world about it via networking, social media, your website/shop/outlet.

Now comes the skills part! I want to highlight two key aspects that I have learned drive my sales business. These are the 'skeletons' that support the structure of the selling the method which I choose to use, called 'Conversational Sales'. How I flesh them out is personal to my style as it will be for yours. Conversational Sales puts the customer at the heart of every sale when Mary Kay Ash first built her company over 50 years ago, she included this quote in every consultant's sales training:

> *"Pretend that every single person you meet has a sign around his or her neck that says 'Make me feel important!' Not only will you succeed in sales, you will succeed in life"*
>
> *Mary Kay Ash*

It is still currently used to help all new consultants better understand how to build a successful sales business built on being customer focussed and building rapport. The result of a Sales Conversation is wanting more than just a one-off purchase.

How do we start a Sales Conversation with a potential purchaser?

There is a Selling Cycle and your skill is finding where your purchaser fits into it, will give you a clue of how to start the conversation and what sort of question to ask first. This a million miles away from the formulaic cold calling type sales that asks one opening question before launching into "sales patter". This is a sincere desire to find out what the customer is looking for and where they are in the decision-making process, and therefore where you and your product 'fit'.

The Selling Cycle: Potential opportunities to interact with customers

For example:

1. Customer recognises a problem/ a need/ a desire/ a dream

2. Customer knows you exist /finds you – visibility through marketing

3. Customer wants to resolve concerns about suitability/ price/ availability/ guarantees/ post-purchase service

4. Customer ready to purchase – why choose you? / now or later

5. Customer wishes to re-purchase – customer service/ referral business/ developing trust

Once you have identified 'where' they are in this cycle, it is easier to have a sales conversation.

Touch Point Sales

The second idea to consider is that of 'Touch Point Sales'. A 'touch' is a positive interaction made by a customer with you and your product. Simply looking at a website does not count, but engaging in an online chat does (information gathering). Signing up for a Newsletter counts. Liking and following your Facebook business page counts. Calling you or your customer service team counts. Sampling your products counts. Reading reviews and testimonials also count. Looking at a billboard advertisement does not count! It is commonly accepted that it takes up to eight or more 'touches' before a potential purchaser will decide to buy from you. Here's the question – can you identify all the opportunities there are to interact with you and your product?

Think backwards! What steps does the customer take, or thoughts do they have before they reach you personally – what can they do to interact and decide that you are the chosen supplier?

– Can they find you by Googling you or your product?

– Do you have a web site?

– Do you have a social media presence on all major platforms?

– Do you have testimonials and reviews available to read?

– What about YouTube? Facebook Live?

Each time someone 'clicks through' it is an interaction. How do you stand out?

– Are you the expert?

– Are you quickly and simply available to connect with?

– Do you answer your mobile phone?

– Do you respond to messages promptly?

List what makes you different:

–

–

–

–

When the customer finds you, what do you offer?

– On-line catalogue and sales service

– Shop/office

– Personal appointment

– Taster session/samples

In my career with Mary Kay Cosmetics we offer 'try before you buy' appointments either one to one or in small groups. That way the customer sees and tries the product with expert guidance and suggestions from the Mary Kay consultant. A very definite interaction and opportunity for three or four 'touch points'.

1.   They meet you as a potential supplier.

2.   They try products that are personalised to their requirements.

3.   They have all questions answered.

4.   They see the cost and value of the product. They enjoy the sales process and are made to feel special.

5.   They are offered an after sales service that is second to none.

6.   They understand they have a 100% satisfaction guarantee on their purchases.

Remember Mary Kay consultants are trained to make every person they meet feel important. It is that invisible sign carried by every potential customer. It is key to good sales.

In your sales experience can you identify at least five 'touch points' right now? Try it:

1.

2.

3.

4.

5.

If you can do that, or at least agree with the theory, you are ready to get going on the Sales Conversation. Remember that Conversational Selling depends on dialogue with your potential customer, not a script. Why the person is contemplating a purchase and where are they in the Selling Cycle described earlier are important to establish. It is only by asking questions about them that you will find the answer!

It's a bit like doing a jigsaw and putting the sales picture together piece by piece! Again, remember to think backwards – what has brought that person to you? What is their need, desire, idea, frustration? Can you solve it? That's where the Sales Conversation starts. Find out about them first:

– "Tell me about you!"

– What are you looking for?

– Have you been looking for a long time?

– Has fate brought us together, or Google?!

These are suggestions not an overpowering list to be fired off:

– Have they got a budget?

– Do they know how much your product costs?

– Is there a timescale?

– Are they going to make a decision today?

As we want customers who re-purchase and refer, I think this 'getting to know you' part of the sales conversation is vital. Make mental notes as you chat. **Be that good listener.**

– Is there a practical part to your sales conversation?

– Do they need to try the product?

– Do they need another appointment before a decision can be made?

– Perhaps they need to talk to someone else about the purchase.

– Maybe they have to make other financial decisions first.

– Have they got other people to see (competitors)?

All these things are likely and normal. By the time the person has reached you they have probably researched a few products or options. What they are looking for will become obvious if you ask enough questions and answer with clarity.

Remember the 'Touch Point' plan. Somewhere after around five interactions the conversation has to move to the practicality of the sale. **Use your intuition**. Ask simple questions such as:

- "Susan it's been great chatting with you and I think I have answered all your questions. Is that right?"

- "I know we have talked about price and I hope you are happy with that?" (Special offer reminder if offered or appropriate.)

- "Did I explain that I take payment by.........?"

- "Do you think you are ready to make a decision now?"

Don't forget that the sale continues until the product is taken home, delivered, posted out, and so on. Therefore it is important that these happen too:

• Delivery options suit the customer.

- The customer is thanked for choosing your product or service.

- A Customer Service promise is made!

- If the product is re-orderable, now is the time to make sure your customer knows how to get in touch with you and how they like to be contacted.

- If your business is in its infancy, ask if your customer would 'Like' your Facebook Page, and if they would feel confident to write a brief testimonial on your web site or LinkedIn profile.

I am not a fan of the phrases 'Closing the sale', and 'overcoming objections'. I think they are old fashioned and masculine sounding. They echo the old sales systems that were heavily scripted and lost any sincere, authentic interest in what the customer wanted. The sale was what was important, and at all costs. Let's move on from that era. If I have done my sales job properly, I am hoping that I have helped the customer find a solution to whatever brought them to me or even tempted them to something they can't resist! I'm not 'closing' anything, rather I'm opening doors to more sales opportunities by having a happy customer.

That phrase 'overcoming objections' I think sounds aggressive, and again I am in sales to answer questions and provide an exceptional product solution. The task is to make sure I have achieved that well enough through Conversational Sales, to offer the customer a simple choice, having listened to and addressed any concerns they may have.

Here is an observation that might be helpful when the time to choose to purchase arrives – there is no scientific research to back up my observation!

At the Moment of Decision

Women	Men
Brain wired like twinkling Christmas tree lights	Brain wired like a searchlight
As all options are weighed up, evaluated and mentally ranked in importance	Simple choice: is this what I want? Do I want it now? Do I need two?
Sensitive to all choices and needs all information first	Give me the details now
Do I trust you?	Is your product successful?
Are there payment options? What is The delivery? What are the guarantees? Can I contact you? How can I contact you?	Can I pay cash?

(Of course none of the above applies to the purchase of shoes or handbags….!!!)

This is the beginning of a relationship with your customer. Make sure it is a positive and professional one. I am a visual thinker, so if you are the same, perhaps the following diagram will help with a flowchart approach to a Sales Conversation:

Great Chatting

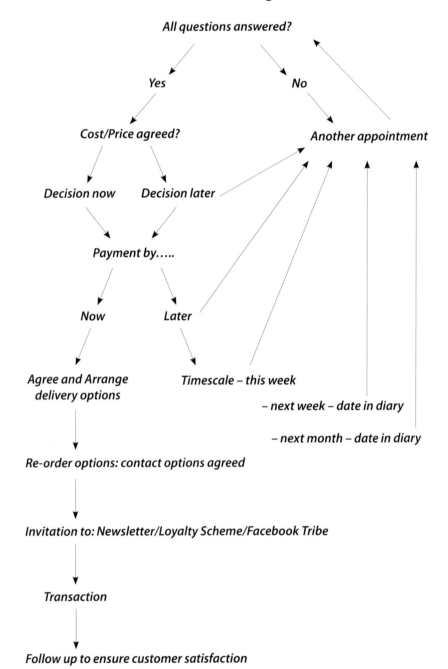

All questions answered?

Yes   *No*

Cost/Price agreed?   *Another appointment*

Decision now   *Decision later*

Payment by…..

Now   *Later*

Agree and Arrange delivery options   *Timescale – this week*

– *next week – date in diary*

– *next month – date in diary*

Re-order options: contact options agreed

Invitation to: Newsletter/Loyalty Scheme/Facebook Tribe

Transaction

Follow up to ensure customer satisfaction

A sales conversation gives the **opportunity to be the nurturer** to develop a professional approachable relationship with the customer. If the customer does not purchase, accept that it is their choice and they haven't chosen your product. As women in sales we do have a tendency to take things personally, and a rejection is not easy. Basically, learning to accept "no thank you" is as much a part of sales as "yes please". We have to put a bit of effort into understanding and expecting rejection of our product and efforts, and realise it is simply that. Our product was not chosen – but what happens next is important for future business!

If the experience is good and person leaves with a good impression of you and your product, they are more likely to speak highly of you to others. And let me assure you that people do return at a later date if they cannot make a decision "at that moment" (Selling Cycle). As sales people it is not our business to know our customer's personal situation. However, that can be far more influential on determining a purchase than anything we say or do. If there is no sales leave them with an invitation, for example:

"Would you like to:

– sign up for my/our Newsletter?

– join my/our mailing list for special offers?

– have my business card for reference?

– be invited to my/our next customer event?

And most importantly, give them a courteous and sincere "Thank you" for their time and interest. The best conversations are the ones that end with both parties happy and perhaps looking forward to another one!

The Red Handbag

As Shakespeare might have said: "How do I buy thee? Let me count the ways!"

I think there are three main reasons why women make purchases:

– Need
– Desire
– Whim

Let me explain a little more how I came to that conclusion! I am fascinated by why people buy, as much as by what they buy. I believe that knowing about the why is crucial in sales at this moment in time. Especially when I want them to choose my products over my competitors.

With the internet at our command, we can research our prospective purchase in minutes if we so desire. We have comparison websites to help find us the best deal. We have Instagram and Pinterest loaded with tempting images. We have YouTube brimming with instructional videos on 'How to....'

We can choose to know as much as the seller about the object of our desire. We formulate lists of priorities to go with the list of requirements. So, what are we left wanting? What delays or speeds the purchase other than the right combination of product, price and timing?

Back to my Top 3 choices for the drive behind the sale. Take note it is a commonly held belief that we buy on emotion and rationalise with logic!

Need

This is the easiest to work out! The shower head breaks and I need a replacement. This may be an irritating purchase as it is urgent, inconvenient and yet necessary. I do an internet search. Simple. I ask my friends for recommendations. I select my best option fairly easily. I dismantle the old shower head and take it with me to the chosen Plumbers' Merchant to pick up a new one. (Feeling quite smug about that bit......the fitting must match the hose!)

Once there I ask to see the item I have selected online, but the wise assistant thinks to show me a second option which in his opinion, might suit my needs better. He has already heard my tale of woe! His suggestion turns out to be an excellent one as it addresses an extra need (problem of low water pressure) that I had not taken into account. (Good sales service).

His suggestion is less expensive than my first choice and comes with a guarantee (product + price).

I am impressed. I buy two because now he has me thinking about the other shower in our house and how that would be improved with a new shower head too (timing).

We are both happy with the transaction. A need/problem solved, a solution found with the extra helping of expertise that ensured the sale.

Desire

I have desired a red handbag for years. My husband is fed up with shopping diversions around handbag shops. I could quite easily fill an hour of time scrolling through choices on the internet, friends' handbags are scrutinised closely if they are red, fashion magazines avidly browsed if they contain articles on handbags. However, I knew that when I actually SAW the handbag, I would know it was THE ONE. My husband does not understand that, but I'm sure he would if it were a car.

It had to be a certain shade of red. It had to be a certain type of smooth leather. It had to have a definite shape. It had to have a definite size. It had to be a classic, I'm talking "leave it in your will" level classic. Price was not a worry as I knew the right handbag would be the perfect price too.

Let's be clear, I did not need a red handbag. I desired a red handbag.

When the perfect handbag at last came into view, in a shop in Italy last year, it was so very exciting. It fulfilled my dreams. The purchase was assured. I think the shop assistant may have been surprised at my obvious delight, or perhaps it was the look of relief on my husband's face? And he was so pleased, probably that the search was over, that he paid the bill!

It ticks all the boxes, makes me smile every time I use it and quite rightly gets compliments whenever we are out and about.

A different sort of sale. I knew exactly what I wanted, and all the sales assistant did was wrap up my bag with a flourish and take the money. No need for suggestions, no attempt to upsell as I was 100% happy, wise move. I will recommend that shop.

Whim

I was attending a special Shopping Event geared very much to women. Lots of opportunities to browse, be tempted, perhaps do a little early Christmas shopping, you know the sort of thing! The stands had gone all out to look attractive and tempting. It was a fun *day out. One of the stands took my eye immediately as first off it was crowded with ladies obviously shopping! Curiosity piqued so I went to see why. And there, displayed enticingly, were the most beautiful candles. They had a unique cone shape, they came in a myriad of colours, there were different sizes so that you could make a stunning display with ease.*

Cleverly the business owner had used seasonal colours for her displays and all at once I could 'see' how my Christmas table would look absolutely perfect with just that display!

I bought the same set of candles that were on display. I also bought the napkins and some cute wine glass decorations to complete my 'vision' because they were displayed near the till!

Whim. No 'need', no 'desire', just instant decision and instant satisfaction.

Afterwards I justified my purchase with a list of very good reasons: price, exclusivity, availability, proximity to Christmas, time saving even, as we tend to do when we make a whimsical purchase!

I also came away with a catalogue and the contact details of the seller who was charming. Now there is an interesting twist, as by the spring I was in touch with her again to select more candles in different shades!

Each of those examples has one common thread. The sale was all about ME the PURCHASER and what was running through my mind. That is the shift in sales today, it is no longer about the seller making the sale, it is all about helping the customer make the purchase. If you are in sales the skill that is required is finding out more about the customer, why they are looking at your product, and then being genuinely helpful and appropriate in your interaction with them. It's almost starting a relationship with the customer that is not dependent on a single sale, but valuing how customer opinion and recommendation can help build your business.

Need, desire or whim? Are you ready to make the purchase a positive one for both of you? We need to tune in to the customer and adapt our sales conversation appropriately.

Searching for the Red Handbag in Montepulciano!

Chapter 5

Are You the Expert?

"Success occurs when opportunity meets preparation"
Zig Zigler

It is an interesting time in Sales. Gone are the days when a sales person would be sought out by the buyer to give information, a brochure with price list, and answer technical questions. The advent of the use of internet search engines and comparison sites now means that, with a couple of clicks, the buyer has potentially as much 'product' knowledge at their fingertips as the seller. Daniel Pink (see references) refers to it as 'Information Parity'. So where do we fit in? And what can we do to secure the sale? What is the customer looking for or expecting?

I think it is really important and valuable to become expert in your product knowledge or a leader in your field of service. Nowadays we are aware that a customer is looking for re-assurance and confirmation of correct choice, built on the research they have already done. They want to know that 'you know your facts' as this builds trust. That you are the 'go to' person who can answer questions as they arise, confirm facts (eg. price and delivery details). Knowing the answer to possible questions, or being to access answers quickly, gives security and confidence in a Sales Conversation. That you are interested in them and in developing a customer/client relationship that results in 'high trust' sales and superb customer service.

How do you become an Expert? It is said that to become an expert takes 10,000 hours of work (who decides these things?). Anyway, that's quite a chunk of time, and whilst admirable, I do not advocate waiting until you've completed 10,000 hours in order to aspire to the title. Certainly make an investment of time to research your product and those of your competitors. Having a student mentality is good; gaining knowledge directly affects your self-confidence.

The world we live in today has changed beyond imagination since I started my sales career and I have no doubt, as technology keeps advancing, it will continue to do so. There are always new skills to learn; don't be fearful, find out what you need to know and build your own expertise. Twenty-six years ago I knew precious little about skincare and make-up, but I was surrounded by people who did and I learned 'my trade' from them.

The learning has never stopped as new exciting products are created all the time which I need to know about if they are to benefit my customers and my business. Twenty-six years ago I did not possess a computer! Now that really did demand a new level of learning and continues to demand attention as technology advances. Ten years ago I knew nothing about social media, or the impact it was going to have on sales and marketing, but I understood I needed to learn all about it. I found someone who did (a 'go to' person) and learned from them.

Of course learning did not end there and, as it is still so influential, to this day I continue to attend workshops and classes to keep my knowledge current. It is part of constructing and maintaining my expertise and confidence. I want my customers to feel confident too when they buy my products. I want them to enjoy using them and to re-order them.

I want them to:

– trust me

– speak positively about my products

– recommend me and my products to their friends and associates

– have the best purchasing experience

– know they are getting expert advice and specialist customer care

What can you add to this list? Where are the areas in which you need to improve, or to help you achieve, or to maintain 'Expert' status?

Once the product knowledge has been learned I think we need to become 'People Experts'. We have completed check-lists for product knowledge, introductions, our image, our expertise, so that we are confident and prepared when we meet our potential customers. We know to find out about them and what they require.

When we start the sales conversation it is all about them. We are looking for clues that tell us more about our customer, so that we can help provide the answers to questions, be respectful of their choices, but also enthusiastic about what we offer to secure the sale. Imagine if there was a simple system that would help you interact with people?

Well there are several such systems, and the one I first met over 20 years ago and have espoused ever since, is the DiSC® system for personality profiling. It is a really simple tool that helps improve communication, build better relationships and increase sales. (As part of my quest to become an 'expert' I became an accredited DiSC® trainer). The system is based on four distinct behavioural styles:

Dominance

Influence

Steadiness

Conscientiousness

Initially you need to discover your own DiSC® behavioural style through a series of questions. Once you learn how to identify the different types, you will be able to recognise their styles and how they relate to yours. In a sales situation you develop a greater awareness and thus understanding of customer styles. This can help you deliver a much better sales conversation.

People with a **Dominance, or D style**, are motivated by results, action, and fast pace. So when communicating you need to be brief, direct and focussed, and produce the answers efficiently.

People with an **Influence, or i style**, are motivated by enthusiasm and action, and visual information. They do not respond well to too much detail, but need to see, feel and talk about the purchase, and enjoy and create excitement. They buy spontaneously!

Steadiness or S style people are motivated by support, structure, and stability. In a Sales Conversation they should not be rushed, and you would need to be clear about customer service and reliability. Such people may be the slowest to purchase, but generally exhibit huge brand loyalty once the choice is made!

Finally, **Conscientiousness or C style** people are motivated by accuracy, quality, clear systems, and definitely expertise! They will expect a clear, detailed approach to any sale and do not rush them – make a second appointment if necessary.

As intuitive women we can be great at working with this tool. I urge you to find out more, complete a profile, and put what you learn to work for you.

Using DiSC® does not mean that we intend to manipulate or use pretence in our sales approach. We are customer-led and it is vital we 'tune in' to what our customers are saying, and in some cases not saying! We have to change our perspective and see the sale from the customer's point of view. Understanding that each customer is likely to fall predominantly into one of the DiSC® behavioural styles allows us the opportunity and sensitivity to accommodate them.

For example, a well-produced product brochure full of attractive images will interest and excite someone with the i style, who is likely to purchase and want immediate delivery or to take it home if possible! Whereas a list in small print of the product's potential, with no pictures, will not have the same impact.

Similarly a **C** behavioural style will require both brochure and price list as well as expecting the Salesperson to answer relevant questions.

The **S** behavioural style will take the brochure and price list home to study, and return with a few questions that need a reassuring answer. During that space of time they will have asked for other opinions.

The **D** behavioural style will probably have made the buying choice from personal research and is seeking confirmation of their decision; the brochure could therefore be irrelevant.

If you/we can be prepared to adapt easily to each of these styles then Sales Conversations, as well as results, will improve. Looking at the DiSC® customer mapping in the circumplex model of emotion[*]

---

[*] *The circumplex model of emotion is a presentation where the emotional variables are arranged in a two-dimensional circular space, containing the dimensions of arousal on the vertical axis, and valence (attractiveness/averseness to a situation) on the horizontal axis.*

"Everything DiSC® Sales: Customer Mapping.
All rights reserved. Used by permission."
(See Further Reading, Inspiration, and Resources)

above, after we have decided our own predominant style, it is useful to note that the style which is opposite to our own will demand more of our effort to establish a positive interaction, compared to the other two.

In conclusion, seek out the experts who will help you improve your skill set, understanding and performance. There is masses of help available and good information to explore. I like to read and re-read so I have included a Reading List at the end of the book. Some titles may be familiar, others new, but they have all struck a chord with me! Elevate yourself to expert status!

Pruning – it has to be done!

We've just finished pruning our olive trees for this year. It is a labour of love and a necessity, demanding concentration and energy. Pruning ensures that the trees are given the best opportunity to thrive and will, we hope, ensure an abundance and easy harvesting of the olives in six months' time. It's a time of assessment, and I find the simple rituals therapeutic and satisfying.

It strikes me that there are parallels between pruning the olives and running my own business. However, though I approach pruning joyfully, understanding the need for what can sometimes be quite brutal and bold actions, I don't seem to have the same enthusiasm for assessing my own business performance!

With that in mind this year, I decided the two would happen at the same time, and maybe the enthusiasm for one job would spill over into the other. The simple truth is that as small business owners we should, and must, review and assess what we are doing. My mentor Anne Newbury always told me to "inspect what you expect". If my business is to grow, flourish and produce profit, it has to move forward not stagnate. 'Nothing wilts faster than a laurel rested upon!'

I know all this – but still I seem reluctant to actually do a business review and even a 'prune' to achieve better results. So it came down to drawing the parallels and going to work on both things!

Part 1 – the olives:

1. What do I want?

– healthy trees
– abundant harvest
– easy picking

2. What can I control?

– height and shape of the trees
– removal of suckers and weeds
– making sure there is light and space between branches for
    optimum climate benefits
– spraying and fertilizing as necessary

Part 2 – my business:

1. What do I want?

– a healthy profitable business
– achieving goals that make my dreams come true

2. What can I control?

– how much I work
– when I work
– where I work
– removal of distractions and detours
– strong sustainable growth built on simple, and appropriate
    (Mary Kay), business principles

3. Do I have the right tools for the job?

– am I up to date on product knowledge?
– am I up to date on small business savvy?

4. *Do I need help? (whether office or home)*

– do I have an active mentor?
– where do I go for advice?

With the olives the work is done in the Spring for harvest results in the Autumn. It is not an instant result. We cut out dead wood, thin out the branches, remove suckers and weeds. We spray and fertilise the trees to protect them from disease and to add extra nutrients, and then we let them grow. The parallels are easy to see for my business and I know I won't see immediate results. However, I know that what I am doing today will get me what I want in the future.

To make my business strong and healthy, I need to follow simple rules. I need to introduce ladies to our products (parties etc) and share opportunity offered by Mary Kay (recruiting and developing a sales team). This is my checklist:

−   *am I meeting enough ladies every week to achieve new sales?*

−   *am I taking proper care of my existing customers?*

−   *am I up to date on product knowledge, using every avenue of learning open to me?*

−   *am I meeting enough ladies every week to hear Mary Kay's story and invite them to join us?*

−   *am I helping my existing team develop their businesses?*

−   *do I need to 'prune' the distractions that prevent me from expanding my business?*

−   *do I need to 'weed out' the people and things that drain my energy and enthusiasm?*

- *do I need to seek out a mentor who will give me good advice and provide 'fertilizer' to boost my business plans?*

- *am I energetic?*

- *am I preparing for and pursuing success and an abundant harvest?*

Doing things this way gave me FOCUS. I want my olives and my business to thrive. They both need my care and attention! Job done! Let's see what this year brings.

Chapter 6

The Impact of Online Selling and Social Media

> *"Social is not a place for a hard sell –*
> *it's a place to build trust and credibility"*
> *Julio Viskovich*

I am not a Digital Native. I am a Digital Immigrant. I have learned how to use what I need to use, and what benefits my business in terms of sales. I understand why I need social media as part of that Selling skill set. As I mentioned, ten years ago I knew nothing of social media and had elementary knowledge of computers. Did any of us truly have an idea of just how extraordinary the combined effect of world wide web and social media was going to impact sales? I certainly did not!

Watching the movie 'The Social Network' reminded me of the sheer speed of change. Like a before and after picture. How quickly purchasing/buying/shopping became a part of this 24 hour global activity, seven days a week, at any time. The influence on buying, because thousands of people had access to tempting images of products they might want at the click of a mouse (or just a click). And how quickly followed the ability to buy the products with another three clicks! In sales, we were playing catch-up, from the "How do we reach customers?", "How do we take payment for products?", "How do we deliver?", "How do we maintain customer service?", to the far more complex "How do we compete in this expanded market?". It has been a steep learning curve!

And now we have an entire generation of 'screen babies' who wouldn't know how to survive without a mobile device and access the internet. They can shop when they want. They can compare products when they want. They can have all the product knowledge to answer every question, and they can have their purchase delivered to their door within days if not hours. We are constantly being reminded of the decline of high street shops, and the unstoppable rise of online shopping. E-commerce is here to stay.

What does it mean for us as sales people? Is it the end of a career option? I think the answer is "No". Why? In my experience however efficient an online sales service is, there is always room for personal connections. It may be in the customer service end of the transaction, but a happy customer is always our aim. Happy customers re-purchase and they happily refer to our products or service to others. Happy customers write glowing testimonials which are worth their weight in gold. We have all been unhappy customers, disappointed by the delivery of a purchase that didn't live up to its on-screen image and description, and wanted to talk to someone about our dissatisfaction! We have all had to arrange returns and refunds that require a call to a Customer Services department. Sometimes only an expert sales person will do when the bright shiny machine won't function, or we want a modification to a design.

It may not be to do with the initial sale, but contact with real people in real time is important to the development of further Sales Conversations with your customer. Remember the invisible sign 'Make me feel important'. Well it's never more important than when you're sorting out a customer problem! And future sales can certainly be impacted and lost by the lack of personal attention and expert help, rather than a Chatbot or Online Query form. (Two words: Budget Airline, should fill your heart with dread!). Having an online presence can help you with lead generation, from good marketing, the introduction of new products to a wider potential market and therefore greater sales opportunities, to increasing your brand popularity and even in researching new products for expansion, or for checking out the competition. In other words, as sales people we have to keep up and keep current.

If you want to establish an online selling business or expand your business to include online sales, you have many choices to make. Those choices will depend on your confidence level, technical ability and probably your budget. E-commerce is developing rapidly with on-line marketplaces being created all the time. Finding the right one for your product or service will take time and energy, and of course there is always a cost implication. It is outside my area of expertise and there is much information readily available to you should you wish to follow that path.

Do I use online selling in my business? Yes, but it is already established by Mary Kay and all I have to do is subscribe to their platform. For all its ease and speed and 24/7 availability I have to tell you one simple fact, my customers still want a personal connection with me. My customers buy from me because I am the expert link between product selection and their final choice. I am the person offering five-star service, not their ipad. My customers trust me as well as my product.

Social Media and Sales

I approach social media and sales with an emphasis on social. I find that it is a crossover area between marketing and sales. I understand it is where customers can interact with you and your brand. I agree that you can build and expand knowledge of your brand with a tribe of followers, likers and friends. I appreciate the role of influencers, bloggers and vloggers and the impact they have on sales through amassing huge followings and subscribers on social media platforms. To ignore it would be fool-hardy. It has its place, but has it yet replaced the field of sales and follow-up and long-term customer satisfaction? What do you think?

On the plus side you can write your own profile without huge financial investment, and personalise your presence through 'live' comment and opinion. The challenge comes in keeping up with change, which is fast and fundamental to the popularity of social media and keeping the 'audience engaged'. It has its own vocabulary, its own slang and shorthand. It is time-consuming, and has the potential for huge distraction.

Which platforms do you already use? Which platforms do your existing customers use, and more importantly potential customers use? I would suggest that you are selective about where you put your time and energies.

This is my choice of platforms with usage details gleaned from http://www.sproutsocial.com:

Facebook – used by all ages, but more by women than men. Facebook is 'historical' and 'pictorial', i.e. 'Look, this happened'; 'Look what I bought'.

Instagram – for photos/video, used less than Facebook and by a younger demographic, and marginally by more women. The home of the Hashtag, and product temptation. #fashion #happy #buyme

Pinterest – images/videos, under 50's, used more by women. Often for inspiration – new product images. A giant scrapbook! A visual event planner useful for things like weddings.

Twitter – words are paramount and limited to short messages, like strap lines on TV News and comment on customer service. Sadly more criticism than praise. Perfect for mobile 'screen-babies'. Used almost equally by a younger demographic of women and men (apparently only 8% of over 65s currently use Twitter).

LinkedIn – designed specifically for the business community. Used by decision makers. Appears more 'masculine' but is used equally by men and women for online business networking. Perfectly acceptable to highlight your accolades and skills.

And so we come to Google and its ever reaching presence in our lives. Everyone with a computer/mobile device/ipad/laptop knows how to use Google to find answers quickly and people and products. Google yourself – what comes up? If nothing, then from a sales perspective I would do something about it by creating a social media presence for you and your product. Your competition will have one.

You probably know all this information and more. I cannot give you direction as to what will work and what won't. However social media is an addition not a replacement for real time – person to person – money changing hands – product being sold and purchased.

For women in business, especially where we ourselves are the USP (Unique Selling Point), nothing beats being with customers face2face, knee2knee, and toe2toe! And as for enjoyment – give me an appointment with a customer any day over an online transaction!

Footnote

It is my observation that the advent of online marketing and sales has led some people to believe they can become armchair millionaires from the comfort of their front room with a computer, a PayPal account and a product to sell. I am not convinced of the truth of this. My successful sustainable business has been built on the loyal customers trusting me, my product and expertise to deliver results. I don't believe it could have been built in isolation. To quote a well-known Cruise Line, you have to 'Get out there'!

To quote Anne Newbury to the tens of thousands of women she mentored to success in Mary Kay:

"Get up!" "Get cute!" "Get out!"

The e-lemon tree!

Life ~ Lemons ~ Lemonade ~ e-lemon tree, or business without Wi-Fi!

When we first bought our home in Italy 10 years ago, the provision of internet was low on the list of priorities, in fact, I don't think it was even on the list, as we didn't have a fully functioning bathroom or kitchen! Gradually as building projects were completed and we began to spend more time in Italy, the topic of Wi-Fi did get tossed around in conversation. However, the house was originally going to be a holiday home and we all know that you ought to have a holiday from the internet too when relaxing, and so it was not given serious consideration.

Eventually the subject did come back and we decided to investigate the options available. Our finest Italian and a dictionary were put to use. The one good thing about the world of Wi-Fi is that most technical words are in English and the Italians have not tried to produce an Italian translation. This makes communication easier!

We asked our neighbours for recommendations, but found that everyone uses different systems. The general consensus was that sometimes it was possible to get a working signal, sometimes it wasn't. In a small rural community it did not command great importance, more a shrug of the shoulders. They do not have the same attitude towards televisions, which are of huge importance because of football and quiz shows.

Our little house is sandwiched between two much taller buildings, might this cause problems? There was only one way to find out and that was to have an engineer come and try to link us up.

It is probably easier if I list the events that followed. Safe to say that each time we tried, we did so with enthusiasm and commitment matched by that of the variety of men who came and went and always preferred to be paid in cash (never with a receipt)! No names will be mentioned until I reach the final instalment (literally):

- *1st Attempt with a new metal dish smartly placed on the roof. A success! Although the signal was not strong and was variable, this happily lasted for at least 2 years until it suddenly it stopped working whilst we were away in England.*

- *Eventually we were told that as we had not used it for a period of time 'the system' decided we no longer wanted to use it, so it ceased to work. Monthly payments had not stopped, but that did not count.*

- *2nd Attempt to re-install the system, which meant approximately 3 phone calls a day for at least a week to a central telephone exchange in Milan to organise an engineer to come and set up. When the man arrived, it seemed that a different design of dish (for which cash payment was expected) was needed. Once again we had an internet signal for Wi-Fi – hurrah!*

- *Our building work now included the enormous upheaval of having the house re-wired and this included having a new tv aerial. We thought we would be able to watch Italian tv, which was helpful to our lamentable language skills, as well as use the internet. We left confident that all was working.*

- *3rd Attempt. On returning from the UK, we found that the internet signal had vanished. More endless phone calls to Milan ensued. Another engineer arrived and reported that the antenna had been "fried" by lightning, but he and his side-kick were confident that they could fix things. We had never anticipated potential problems from thunderstorms and lightning strikes! Of course another design of dish, less susceptible to lightning was needed (cash payment naturally). We also noticed, with some concern, that they attached the new dish with plastic tape to the tv aerial post, but they seemed confident and the system worked. The tv however was temperamental, until my husband noticed whilst squinting at the roof, that they seemed to have moved the tv aerial direction!*

- *Reader, it lasted but weeks before the internet packed up after a very strong gale, and so did our ability to access any television channels. We made the decision then and there that we would abandon all hope of having a fully functioning system, and that it was cheaper to drive to town to the local Coffee Shop with free Wi-Fi than continue with the on-going saga that we seemed to have created.*

- *I paid for whatever extra phone data I needed to use to keep my business running smoothly, invested in a very smart phone and worked out how to use a Hot-Spot, even though it felt as though I was single-handedly boosting O2's annual profits.*

- *4th Attempt! 2 years later.......... Missing the daily news in Italian and having realised that my business now totally needed the ability to stay connected via Wi-Fi, combined with our increasing dependence on Wi-Fi telephone calls to family and friends, we decided on ONE LAST TRY. Enter the new service from EOLO.it and Matteo.*

- *As I type it is working perfectly. Yes! Everything has been changed and we have a new dish pointing in a very different direction as this internet signal comes via radio waves. No cash changed hands, it is part of the set-up package! All our tv channels work! We are holding our breath, but Matteo inspired us with his efficiency, knowledge and competency.*

We now enjoy coffee at the coffee shop! All communications with the rest of the world are seamless. My business stress levels are non-existent as I can access everything I need to access at whatever time. Paying a monthly contract is not as expensive as constantly buying bolt-ons every trip!

Why the "e-lemon" mentioned in the title? Well we have simply wonderful neighbours who constantly take care of us when we are here, and our home when we are not here. They were more than happy to share their working internet with us, but you know how it is if you are used to being independent. And truly we did not want to be knocking on their door and "sponging" their signal. However, we did find a couple of things that meant no intrusion into their lives. One was that my husband's phone picked up their Wi-Fi signal automatically at random times if he was outside on our terrace (mine did not). My phone on the other hand, would automatically pick up messages and downloads from their Wi-Fi when I passed the lemon tree at the end of their drive.

And so was born the comment "I'll just stop by the e-lemon and pick up my messages!"

Our Italian Wi-Fi adventure has been along the lines of that well know saying: "When life gives you lemons, make lemonade!" and has taken my sense of humour to its limit at times, but as with many challenges in this life, you have choices. You can give in to frustration and give up, or you can regroup and keep going. You can look for the good things or feel sorry for yourself. We have no idea if we have found the answer to our Wi-Fi woes or not, but writing this has made me smile. Living in, and working from, another country was always going to throw up a few problems, but we've managed and technology is an incredible thing. Perhaps we have just had to allow time to catch up with the advances?

I miss the e-lemon pauses and still find myself dawdling past the end of the neighbour's drive! Old habits die hard, but I am overjoyed with my new dish, my new aerial, my daily dose of Italian tv news, and am positively rapturous about my Wi-Fi download speed!

Chapter 7

Customer Connections

> **"Success in dealing with people depends on a sympathetic grasp of the other person's viewpoint"**
> *Dale Carnegie*

In our current customer focussed Sales Conversations Dale Carnegie's words are 100% true.

We are women in sales cultivating and learning about what is important to us:

– Belief in product

– Outer image

– Mindset and attitude

– Selling techniques

– Personality profiling

We are ready to reach more customers with our product or service. How do we find customers? If you Google that question and avalanche of answers appears. With a brand-new business, you have probably thought – who is going to be interested in buying? Your marketing is created around that target audience. An established business will also have times when it needs to reach a new group of customers to thrive and expand.

In my world of direct selling we know that we need a constant supply of new customers because the choice of products in the cosmetics industry is, as with other sectors, huge. Women make different choices! Fortunately, everyone has skin, so everyone is a prospect. A 'potential' list is helpful because it gets the brain cells going and encourages you to broaden your horizon. Do not pre-judge. Write the heading and then attach a name if possible. Do write the list and preferably in a note book you keep for that purpose. Update your list frequently.

Have you tried all of these examples:

1. Family and relations

2. Friends and social circle

3. Social media

4. Networking groups

5. Sales exhibitions

6. Local organisations (eg. Women's Institute, Rotary, Round Table)

7. Schools – PTA activities

8. Charities and Fund raisers

9. Work colleagues if appropriate

10. Sports groups

11. Local press

12. Joint ventures with local businesses

It is not that you are going to sell to all of them, but are you prepared to chat about what you do or the product you sell, if given the opportunity? Remember social media is a really simple way of letting people know what you are doing and gives an easy conversation starter. Offering to donate, have a stall, give a talk, offer a few freebies to any of that list as a way of opening the Sales Conversation and "going fishing" for prospective customers who show an interest.

Another uncomfortable old-fashioned phrase I dislike is "cold calling" almost as much as "warm chatting". I know that the former is much used by tele-sales companies, but those companies always use scripted calls too. Cold calling does not fit with Conversational Sales. Warm chatting, apart from sounding a little "seedy" also points to a random selection of people who are innocently going about their daily business, being accosted. The worst example of this I can think of is the young people employed by charities to warm chat people in the street to encourage signing up to make donations. As I said, I dislike both approaches and so I choose not to do them or promote them. Generating leads and contacts is necessary, good marketing is key. Being prepared to talk about what you sell with ease is really important. What you are looking for is opportunity and interest! In my mind, looking for new customers is akin to going fishing. You have to cast the net wide to try to improve the catch.

I like to use a description I heard many years ago, used by Emma Wimhurst when thinking about customers, that they fall into three groups:

Strangers, Friends, and Lovers.

Strangers – prospective customers you have yet to meet or find.

Friends – people who have bought your product and are satisfied with it and you. We value them! They are potential Lovers.

Lovers – customers who re-purchase, love your product, love you, appreciate your customer service and tell their friends. A referral gold mine.

Let's talk about these *Strangers*. It is not so much finding customers (you've made the list) as much as being prepared for finding them daily all around you as I mentioned. This preparation includes that 60 second introduction we talked about creating in Chapter 4. Being prepared means carrying your business cards at all times – a brochure or materials about your business to give away. It includes knowing your own availability for booking sales appointments immediately and within the next two weeks and asking enough relevant questions to see if there is a future in the connection. Most important of all is deciding *YOU WILL ALWAYS FOLLOW UP* on any contacts made to develop business.

Just to clarify this, a *Lead* is a *Stranger* you meet who shows interest in your product. That's all. You may give them literature e.g. sales/ exhibition work. Leads only become *Contacts* when personal contact details are exchanged. *Contacts* need to be followed up within 48 hours or you have to start again with business introductions.

In my opinion the most successful sales people never overlook or miss the opportunity to 'collect' sales prospects on a daily basis. The follow-up on the prospect is where the focus should be. Merely collecting names is not enough, neither is adding contact details. Being able to note down why that prospect deserves a follow-up is key. For example:

> ....I sell bathroom fixtures. I meet 'Joanna' at a networking meeting. She mentions she would love a new bathroom. I ask her what her dream bathroom would be like (and make a mental note of the answer). I give her my business card and offer to help make the dream come true. Has she a business card to swap? I ask her if she has a timescale for the new bathroom. Conversation ends with her answer...........

This gives me her contact details to follow up, but more importantly an idea of why my products might interest her. I follow up in a conversational manner. It may be text, email, phone or even via social media. I would acknowledge meeting her. Say something about the meeting (to remind her). Tell her I've noted her plans and timescale for her dream bathroom. Seed the idea that you hope she will make contact when the time is right. Make some suggestions of products that I think would interest her while she is planning and perhaps end the chat with a "see you at the next meeting" type comment. Customer focussed comment. Remember Touch Point Sales. Remember most potential customers do their own product research. Remember you want to be the 'Go To' person. You are creating a few 'touches' to point her in your direction.

Here are some interesting statistics about sales:

> 48% of sales people never follow up with a prospect

> 25% of sales people make a second contact and stop

> 12% of sales people only make three contacts and stop

Only 10% of sales people make more than three contacts

2% of sales are made on the first contact

3% of sales are made on the second contact

5% of sales are made on the third contact

10% of sales are made on the fourth contact

80% of sales are made on the fifth to twelfth contact

'*Strangers* are *friends* you don't know yet'. We could adapt this in this context to '*Strangers*' don't know your products yet. Not all *strangers* will become *friends*, but those that do are deserving of confirmed special attention in business terms.

Friends of our products deserve as much attention as when they were *Strangers*. In fact more, because they now get to experience not only our product but also our customer service. This is why we deliver the best customer service they have ever had supporting our product and giving them total confidence and satisfaction. Not just the 'How did we do?' customer service phone call, not the 'please fill in a satisfaction survey' message, and not being automatically put on an email Newsletter list.

If you run your own business you can make decisions about the following which are all part of Customer Service:

How do you wrap your product at point of sale?

Do you make your postal delivery look exciting?

Do you write personal thank you notes?

Do you remember personal details like birthdays and anniversaries?

Do you have special offers for customers?

Have you created a Loyalty card for re-purchases?

Do you use their name as they wish to be addressed? (No, I do not want to be called by my first name by customer services – ever!).

Do you ask their opinion and listen to the answer?

Do you update them ahead of change?

If you sell for someone else, think how you can make sure that all of the above are considered. And if all your answers are positive – here's a last question, with thanks to the inimitable Geoff Ramm:

> *If a member of the Royal Family, or a Hollywood A-Lister, purchased your product, would your customer service alter?*

Mary Kay Cosmetics currently ranks Number 5 among the global cosmetics brands. I believe this is largely due to our exceptional customer service which Mary Kay Ash called *"And then some"*. We have a re-order and referral customer base that is the envy of the cosmetics industry.

Your *'And then some'* customers are the ones who become *Lovers* of your product. They are the ones who sing your praises, tell their friends, write reviews, give testimonials, and help you build a successful business. They 'sell' for you. They are the proverbial Pot of Gold and are indeed to be treasured. An elite group and I can only imagine the lengths you go to in order to keep them happy! If you've ever experienced an upgrade to fly First Class, a complimentary room change to a suite, a chauffeur rather than the bus, even an 'All areas' backstage Pass, then I think you're getting close to how your product *Lovers* need to be valued.

Kicking up Leaves

Do you remember what it was like to kick up leaves? That feeling of total pointless joy? The feeling that nothing mattered, nothing got damaged or broken, and that it felt so good just kicking. The noise of crunching leaves, the bright colours, the moment in time of letting go! The satisfaction of physical energy released before a return to controlled organised behaviour.

We work in a fast-paced industry. Sales have to be found, customers cared for, sales teams trained, inspired, mentored. Products memorised, company challenges remembered in detail, phone calls made, leads followed up, questions answered. The we have to make time to make it look effortless. Read the trade magazines, write Newsletters, check emails, check the website, check that there is food in the fridge for the next meal. And so on.

Sometimes it feels like twisting an elastic band round your finger…… at first it doesn't really do anything; but after a while the tension begins to exert pressure. A few more twists and it begins to cut off the blood, and your finger feels peculiar. A few more twists and your finger begins to look a funny colour and hurt! If you don't let the tension go you know you will eventually damage the finger!

A little pressure is a good thing. The adrenalin gets you moving. A deadline focuses the mind. We can normally fit everything we want into the day. We utilise all that we are trained to do. We have faith, family and career in harmony.

We write the Six List* of jobs to do and attempt to follow it through. We hang out with positive people. We prioritise. We only moan to those who can put us back on track, or who can restore our vision if we get distracted.

But some days it just doesn't work. The elastic band twists. The family demands block the career, and faith is all that holds it together. The elastic band twists. The appointment cancels, the new team member wants your time but does not match it with her effort. Another twist. The customer returns product because of a "dreadful problem" that seems linked to their bank balance rather than anything else. It's hurting now.

Let it go! Stop whatever you're doing. Find air, be outside, breathe and change your focus for a few moments.

You are in the right place. Your faith will support you as long as you believe. Your family love you whatever you do. Your career will pay dividends as long as you understand the sales model. Your team members will always want more of you. Your customers will appreciate all you do for them, but somehow never quite tell you. "All will be well and all will be well" (St. Julian of Norwich).

Sometimes it is best to just go and kick up leaves!

---

*   *The successful 'Six List Method' was invented by Ivy Lee in 1918 to help businesses to achieve peak productivity.*

At the end of each working day write down the six most important things you need to accomplish tomorrow. Do not write down more than six tasks.

Prioritise those six items in order of their true importance.

When you arrive tomorrow, concentrate only on the first task. Work until the first task is finished before moving on to the second task.

Approach the rest of your list in the same fashion. At the end of the day, move any unfinished items to a new list of six tasks for the following day.

Repeat this process every working day.

Chapter 8

Money and Business

> **"If you are not making money, you have to understand you have an expensive hobby"**
> *Mary Rose Selman*

There is nothing wrong with having an expensive hobby, but the trouble comes if you are pretending it's a business. Similarly, if you are not paid adequately for the job you do for someone else, are you simply volunteering your time and should you look for another job? It would seem wrong to write about selling and sales without talking about money. It is after all what we are trying to make by selling at a profit. Running your own business brings the responsibility for your own Finance Department. Simply put, where the money comes from and where the money goes (cash flow).

> **"If you don't get a handle on the money, where it comes from and goes, you are a wandering generality"**
> *Nancy Boucher*

A reminder of the basic business cycle:

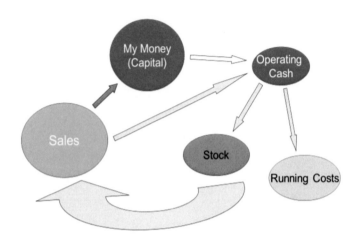

I cannot comment on product pricing, or on how you cost out your business. What I do know is that poor cash flow can cripple a new business and stunt the growth of an existing one. Here are some simple questions to answer to help with money focus:

1. Have you separated your personal banking from your business? If not, why not?

2. Do you allow suitable money from every single transaction for running costs, re-purchasing stock items and re-investment in new product developments, continuous personal development, ongoing developments and tax?

3. Have you studied the HMRC Government web site for initial tax guidance?

4. Do you make physical note of all business expenditure? Are you receipt obsessed?

5. Do you pay yourself something regularly even if it is only enough for a cup of coffee?

6. Do you always have a sales target with a time limit? My wise friend, Nancy Boucher as quoted above, has always taught her sales teams to have sales targets and financial goals in order to keep their business focus.

7. Do you have a financial goal attached to a personal dream? It could be a holiday, a new car, something to celebrate as a family, but start saving towards it. On the 'duvet day' a dream commitment will get you up and out of the door whatever the weather or your mood.

8. Do you have payment systems that suit the customer as well as you? Cash is easy, Bank Transfer is simple. Chip and Pin is necessary. Online may be a solution. And people still write personal cheques.

9. Do you insist that product does not move without payment first? In fact this could be number one on this list.

10. Can you discuss business money matters without becoming emotional, nervous, tense, crying?

If you sailed through all the questions answering "Yes", I salute you. If not, I completely empathise because it took me quite a while to get myself sorted out. I wish I had had that list! The great thing about working nowadays as a small business owner is the amount of niche service help that is available to us. If the answer to a lot of those questions was no, maybe it is time to get help? Why not consider outsourcing your financial management or business administration? There are many small business administration companies (often run by women) who will remove a lot of headaches for you at reasonable cost.

Having done my own book-keeping and tax return for years, I can remember deciding that I needed an accountant. It gave me a feeling of achievement that my business needed that level of expertise, not to mention the amount of time it freed for me to actually expand my business confidently. I chose to get help in the home because it was a better financial choice to pay someone to do the jobs that needed to be done whilst I built a business that could not only pay for that help, but gave another woman a job too. As an aside to this story, the wonderful Louise went on to help me in my office and due to the skills and confidence she developed, started her own separate business.

Do you know how much money your business makes? If you don't know the answer then it makes the question of "is it profitable" impossible to answer. You can do something about it. It starts with a decision to get to grips with it. By mastering simple basics, starting with cash flow, even with simple three column accounting, you will feel better about your business. If you choose to expand and require external investment, you have the groundwork laid to show potential investors. If you expand and need to employ staff to help you, you will know when you can afford to time the expansion. It is just good old-fashioned common sense to 'get a handle' on the money!

When it is organised, the idea of setting sales targets becomes much easier. I am a firm believer in having sales targets, annual ones and then breaking it down into monthly and weekly goals. I urge you to have a financial sales goal in figures. I am not suggesting a random figure. All the women I have worked with want money for a purpose, for example:

– to improve the family budget

– to have holidays

– to provide some education

– to provide care home costs

– to fund a charitable foundation

– to boost a pension plan or provide one

We understand that our business success is shown by our profits. As women in sales and in business, it is my opinion that there has to be a purpose for the profit. What do we want to do with our profits? And what is the figure attached to that answer? What is the sales implication? It's a simple system to help you define a sales goal. It never ceases to amaze me that a sales goal written down is far more likely to be achieved than being kept like a shameful secret. More and more studies show that people who have a goal are more successful than those who do not have one. Write that goal down and you are increasing the chances of the brain automatically recalling it. The encoding gives the goal added importance.

> *"The faintest ink is better than the most retentive memory"*
> *Mary Kay Ash*

And finally, a word about when a hobby becomes a business. Current advice (April 2019) is that a hobby may be classed as a business by the Inland Revenue for tax purposes if the gross annual income is greater than £1,000. Below that figure you do not have to pay any tax, or register for self-assessment. Interesting point is that you may claim 'Allowable' expenses and losses against a registered business, but this does not apply to a Hobby. The HMRC website (http://www.gov.uk) is excellent and full of valuable information that is easily accessible, especially for Sole Traders.

I also agree with the quote:

"Treat your business like a business and it will pay you like a business"

Finding Your Way

Marrakech, a city of sounds and sizzling colour, of souks and sights and shopping. Warm sunshine in wintry months. Perfect for a few days break from the wettest winter for years. Perfect for a complete change and therefore a rest with the added promise of culture and retail therapy.

Mint tea and rose petals greeted our arrival at the Riad el Zohar where we were staying in the centre of the city. The charm of our hosts added to the warm welcome and the generous offer to show us around.

"We will take you out and show you the way back".
"Don't worry, you will get lost!"
"Carry our phone number and call if you need us to come and find you".

Now going out and getting lost is not on my daily 'to do' list, nor has it ever been part of any goal setting exercise I have undertaken! Getting lost implies a loss of control, something fearful, perhaps careless, not a planned activity, definitely to be avoided. So, we had two choices – go out or stay in.

'In' was lovely with its roof terrace and sun loungers, or a more than comfortable bedroom, book-lined sitting rooms and a delightful courtyard and of course endless mint tea on request. 'Out' was the exciting temptation of shops and stalls and good old-fashioned curiosity about a new city with thousands of years of history.

So out we went with our guide! It was a simple route, albeit through a winding alleyway, to the street which then led to the main square. The key was an archway at the end of the alleyway with three steps. We needed to remember that landmark. Confidently we left our guide and headed off into the souk, making the mental note of the three steps and the archway.

Marrakech was all it promised to be and a couple of hours passed in the blink of an eye before we decided to head for home. Down the street, finding the archway with three steps, we turned into the alleyway. And then we got lost! We knew we were minutes away from our Riad and so we back-tracked to the three steps and started again. No fearfulness, just frustration. And this time we found where we had gone wrong and all was well. So having been lost and found and survived, we planned our next few days around all the things that we wanted to see and do. We walked everywhere. Every day we got lost at some point as it truly is a city of alleyways which all look the same and yet different. But we also always found our way 'home' every day having had the pleasure of experiencing palaces, tombs, souks and cafes, all absorbing and fascinating.

And getting lost meant that we also opened our eyes and ears and became more observant of everything around us. Getting lost wasn't fearful, it was funny, because try as hard as we could to find our way home without getting lost, we failed! We did have to ask for help once or twice, but mostly we found our way back on our own. In many ways it added to our Marrakech holiday. We experienced more than we anticipated. We created more memories of a special time. We certainly had more storied to tell!

It made me reflect that in today's fast-moving world we are encouraged to make plans – set goals – complete daily lists of activities – be sure of our 'pathway to success'. Yet how many of us manage to achieve all of that and what happens when we deviate from the plan and get a bit lost? Do we panic? Do we feel fearful of what may happen next? Do we feel failure?

Well, I am at an age where I know for sure that nothing is for sure. Life is just not like that, but God's delay is not his denial. Don't get me wrong, I have plans and goals. I occasionally complete a 'to do' list! Along the way I have times where the plans have been abandoned as life threw up its challenges. I have had to let go and feel lost. But much like Marrakech, you can find your way back. Sometimes you can do it on your own, sometimes you need to ask for help. Life's detours often provide experiences that surprise us and enrich our lives. It was well worth getting lost every day in Marrakech to remind myself of these simple facts.

A practical 30 days of sales motivation ideas for leaders to use with their sales teams

"It is not the employer who pays the wages.
Employers only handle the money.
It is the customer who pays the wages"
Henry Ford

Building a sales team within Mary Kay Cosmetics has been one of the great joys of my career. Helping other women build successful businesses is a privilege. Understanding that a career in sales might not be for them to pursue, but learning all the confidence-building skills associated with sales, will positively impact whatever they choose to do.

A 30 day motivation and selling blitz builds momentum, confidence, expertise, camaraderie, and profit. Not to be done relentlessly, but once or twice a year maybe January and September. Based on the team taking one hour per day – *a power hour* – to focus on their sales business.

Day 1 – Explore Product Information Day.

Are you current and up to date on the products you are offering?

How do our products fit in with what is currently on the market/ in fashion?

Do you have a favourite?

Day 2 – Set a sales goal in £££.

How much profit do you need this week? Is it save or spend?!

Do you have enough sales appointments to support the profit goal?

Have you set aside enough time to succeed?

Day 3 – Seeing is believing and achieving.

This is fun – trash the house and office with posters/post-its/ pictures of what you are aiming to spend your profits on (now or later).

Tell your family and pets what your plan is.

Don't question it, do it. Your brain goes to work on what it sees automatically! The constant reminders help your subconscious work towards the goal.

Day 4 – Expand your thinking then act!

Where is new business coming from? New contacts, referrals from customers, focussed marketing, networking leads?

How often do you think, but not do? What could change to get you in front of more people?

Are you enthusiastic? Enthusiasm sells!

Remember the last four letters – iasm:

$i = $ I

$a = $ am

$s = $ sold

$m = $ myself

Day 5 – Know the numbers.

5.3.1 = 5 invitations to new potential customers.
    3 will agree to try/sample/sit down with you.
    1 (or 2) will be a yes please sale.

5-8 touchpoints to a sale – where are they?

50% will buy and **50%** will not!

No surprise = no stress

Day 6 – Do the figures.

Where does your business come from in percentage terms?

New

Existing

Casual

Online

Once you know, you can direct your energy and focus.

Are there gaps that you can fill? Markets to explore?

Day 7 – Check your social media.

What's working, what is not?

Is your feed up to date?

Are you brave enough to go 'live'?

Day 8 – Celebrate your victories.

Two appointments held?

Sales target reached or exceeded?

New customers joining your list? You need the 'Strangers' so you can make 'Friends'!

Time for a TREAT!!

Day 9 – At the heart of your business is SALES.

Stop selling and everything stalls.

A sales target keeps you focussed – revisit your new one.

Do you have at least two future sales appointments in the diary? If not, go book them.

Day 10 – Information Parity.

Your customer can fact check everything themselves. Sales becomes more about matching the right product to the customer requirement.

What questions are most important to ask? Write them down!

Listen not tell. You're building a customer relationship.

Day 11 – Reconnect with customers.

Build a referral business. Who can you ask? Which customers are your 'Lovers'?

Build or expand your V.I.P. customer group today: 'Make me feel important' – the invisible sign.

Customers for life based on high trust sales.

Day 12 – Be a student day.

Read something that boosts your business, something positive.

Listen to something that gives you joy.

Find time for quiet thought to encourage calm.

Day 13 – Power hour of personal development.

What makes you tick?

Re-write the story you're telling yourself. Highlight your accomplishments.

Shape the way you think with positive vibes.

"No's" don't matter, what's important is to ask.

Don't expect people to understand your dream. 'What you think about you bring about'.

Day 14 – Time to make new connections.

Check these out: More 'Strangers' to meet!

Networking groups

Church groups

Social groups

Facebook groups

School groups

Exercise groups

Day 15 – Celebrate with those you love.

Time to treat everyone with your sales profits. They're your support team, say thank you.

Create a special offer for your V.I.P. customers.

Donate to your preferred charity.

Day 16 – Half-way share.

Share your best sale with the team.

Share your funniest sales story with the team.

Share your top tip with the team.

Day 17 – Double up day!

Book four appointments.

Double last week's sales target.

Connect with two new people <u>today</u>.

Day 18 – What do you love about selling your products?

Write down your three favourite comments from customers.

What do you love about what you sell?

What's the best compliment from a customer you've received?

Day 19 – Today is all about NEW!
Don't overthink or pre-judge, just go for it!

New leads.

New contacts.

New customers.

Day 20 – Winning is good for you! It reinforces effort and completion of action. And it makes you feel good.

Look for the opportunity to win.

Enjoy being a winner.

Be an active participant in a winning team.
Together Everyone Achieves More.

Day 21 – What's your purpose? Define it.

What gets you into action and out of the door?

To whom have you made a commitment that you won't break?

Your purpose must be bigger than your problem.

Day 22 – Review Day. Think about the last seven days' sales.

What are you going to: – keep and repeat. Highlight.

– ditch and delete. Cross out.

– tweak and improve. Edit.

Day 23 – Ask for help day.

Who do you know who is where you would like to be? Contact them and then ask if they would mentor you.

A problem shared is a problem halved.

Is something holding you back?

What's frustrating you right now?

Day 24 – Create a special offer.

Customer appreciation day! Prize draw! Everyone's name in the hat!

Lucky follower on Facebook – create a competition.

Make a caption competition with a product photo.

Day 25 – Become the expert.

Why are we better than the competition?

What is our USP?

Write a list of 'Little known facts' about our product's history.

Day 26 – Write a blog day! If you've never done it, give it a try. Here are some topics. Post it on LinkedIn.

Why my customers buy my products.

What's the difference between a feature and a benefit?

Why women buy on a whim!

Day 27 – 'Go fishing' day.

Try a completely new market.

Check through all your new followers on Facebook/Instagram and message them a thank you, and ask for a referral.

Create a product board on Pinterest that reflects the season.

Day 28 – Pay a compliment day. Well, pay lots of sincere compliments.

How many people can you reach?

Develop an attitude of gratitude.

Happiness is contagious.

Day 29 – Start your review of the 30 day blitz.

Have you increased sales?

Have you increased your customer base?

Are you feeling more confident?

Day 30 – Have you formed new success habits?

Always have a sales target.

Always have appointments.

Be prepared for change.

Stick to your purpose.

Be grateful.

Always follow up.

Gathering Walnuts

Thank heavens I didn't have that manicure!

The phrase 'Do the things you have to do today, in order to choose the things you do tomorrow' keeps coming back to me. Was it from Mary Kay or Anne Newbury? I can't honestly remember but right now, this minute, I am choosing what I want to do because for years I have had the discipline to do what I had to do! I am so glad that I did!

I am enjoying the abundance of God's harvest gathering walnuts from a very old tree, on a very old hillside, where we are fortunate to have a house in Umbria, Italy.

The house is something of a Mary Kay dream come true. If I had not joined Mary Kay over 20 years ago, my life would have been very different. I would have stayed a teacher and we would have stayed in our house until we retired. Probably very contentedly! But having decided that becoming a Mary Kay Director was the career path I wanted to pursue, change was inevitable. I embarked on a life of opportunity where with effort, goals became signposts to success and dreams became a reality. A life where I was positively encouraged to expand my thoughts, to stretch my talents, to have a vision of the future which no-one would ridicule.

The little house in Italy is a culmination of how Mary Kay's vision has influenced our family life. A house in Italy was one of my very first stated dreams and a fading photo was pinned to the 'fridge' door for many years. And now here we are. It took 15 years for the dream to become reality, but it is so worth it!

As for gathering walnuts, well it is a practical activity and it does remind me about finishing a job once it's started! It would be easier if there were two of us! One could shake the tree and the other could see where they fall in the long damp grass. But hey ho, there is only me and so I get on and pick up what I can see, and then expand the search for the walnuts that have fallen and rolled a distance. They all need to be gathered.

Walnuts come in all sizes! As do the daily tasks we have to do whilst building a business.

Walnuts can look perfect…..like shop-bought; but more often than not they are wrapped in wrinkly black coats that you have to peel off to reveal the nut. Sometimes the easiest looking tasks take the longest to complete.

Sometimes walnut cases peel easily, sometimes it is a struggle. You never know if the nut is going to be sweet and beautiful or bitter and disappointing. Sometimes it is just plain rotten. You just never know unless you try them out, and they all deserve a chance!

Peeling walnuts breaks your nails and stains your fingers. The manicure will have to wait. But the satisfaction at the end of the afternoon; the excitement of spreading them out to dry, and the anticipation of delicious feasts over the next few months, sharing them with others, makes it all worthwhile. The nails will grow and the stains will fade. Starting a business and running it yourself means that at the beginning you roll up your sleeves and do all the jobs. There are days when you wonder why you did it and you learn to deal with challenges you never considered, but there is also the heady sense of freedom and the immense satisfaction of making it work.

I am grateful. Grateful for God's bounty and beauty exemplified by our walnut tree. Grateful to my family for allowing me to follow a dream. Grateful that I chose to start a business with Mary Kay and to the women who have gone before me, shared their experience with me, mentored me, directed me, and cajoled me into doing what I had to do on a daily, weekly, monthly, yearly basis!

Picking the walnuts from your own tree beats buying them any day! The satisfaction of a full basket of nuts to eat is worth the labours of the harvest. It is a pleasure and a privilege to choose to do what I want to do.

Further Reading, Inspiration and Resources

Mary Kay Ash (2008) *The Mary Kay Way – (Timeless principles from America's greatest woman entrepreneur)*, John Wiley and Sons, Hoboken, New Jersey.

Mary Kay Ash (2019) *Mary Kay on People Management – (Timeless principles from America's greatest woman entrepreneur)*, Mary Kay Inc., Dallas.

Anne Newbury (2015) *Gumption, Grit, and Glitter – (Decisions I made to succeed the Mary Kay way)*, Mary Kay Inc., Dallas.

Tara Mohr (2015) *Playing Big – (A Practical Guide for Brilliant Women Like You)*, Arrow Books, London.

Daniel Pink (2013) *To Sell Is Human – (The surprising truth about persuading, convincing, and influencing others)*, Canongate Books, Edinburgh.

Lucy Whittington (2015) *Find Your Thing – (How to discover what you do best, own it and get known for it)*, Capstone, John Wiley, Chichester.

Bella O'Hara (2019) *Focus – (How to Unleash Your Potential)*, http://www.feelgreat2bproductive.com.

Helyn Connerr (2016) *Fish Can't Climb Trees – (Capitalise on your brain's unique wiring to improve the way you learn and communicate)*, Watkins Publishing, London.

Karen Skidmore (2019) *True Profit Business – (How to play your bigger game without burning out)*, Practical Inspiration Publishing, Bramley.

Doyin Olorunfemi (2018) *Grow with Goals – (A step-by-step guide to setting and achieving positively-impacting goals)*, http://www.doyin.co.uk

Pat Williams, Ruth Williams and Michael Mink (2003) *How To Be Like Women Of Influence – (Life lessons from 20 of the greatest)*, Health Communications Inc, Deerfield Beach, Florida.

Jim Underwood (2003) *More Than A Pink Cadillac – (Mary Kay Inc.'s nine leadership keys to success)*, McGraw-Hill, New York.

Geoff Ramm (2015) *Celebrity Service – (Discover the gap in your service you never knew existed)*, Creative Juice Publishing, http://www.geofframm.com.

Emma Wimhurst (2009) *Boom! – (7 disciplines to control, grow and add impact to your business)*, Diva Publishing, Chandlers Ford.

Patrick J. McGiniss (2016) *The 10% Entrepreneur – (Live your startup dream without quitting your day job)*, Portfolio/Penguin, New York.

Daniel Gross (1996) *Forbes® Greatest Business Stories of All Time – (20 Inspiring tales of entrepreneurs who changed the way we live and do business)*, John Wiley & Sons, Inc.

The Fruitful Toolbox is a UK based Authorized Partner for Wiley, supplying and training people to use Everything DiSC®. They provide official Everything DiSC® certification programmes, Everything DiSC® profiles, and facilitated personal learning experiences that are based on the Everything DiSC® model. http://www.fruitfultoolbox.com, Bromsgrove, UK.

Everything DiSC® and Everything DiSC® Sales, ©2014 by John Wiley & Sons. Everything DiSC®, Everything DiSC® Sales, and DiSC® are registered trademarks of John Wiley & Sons. All rights reserved. Permission to reprint granted by John Wiley & Sons. For more information on Everything DiSC®, please visit www.everythingdisc.com.

DiSC® Personality Profile – DiSC® is a personality assessment tool, published by John Wiley & Sons Inc., used to improve work productivity, teamwork, and communication, http://www.discprofile.com.

Direct Selling Associations – http://dsa.org.uk ; http://seldia.eu ; http://dsa.org in the USA ; and the World Federation of Direct Selling Associations http://www.wfdsa.org

Of lemons.......never give up on a dream!

When we bought our home in Italy, we inherited a lemon tree. It was not very well; in fact I think it was left behind to wither and die. But I had never grown or owned a lemon tree! I had a vision of beautiful bright yellow fruit hanging from every branch; the sunshine fruit of Italy everyone expects! My neighbours had lots of them, why not me too?

And so the forgotten lemon has been nurtured and loved; re-potted, fertilised, pruned, spoken to gently, repositioned and wrapped up every winter to protect its branches from cruel Umbrian frosts, and unwrapped every Spring to feel the warmth of sunshine and rain to nourish it.

Over the last seven years we have never given up on the care, but we have never had the abundance of lemons that were my dream. Until this year – and lo and behold there are 43 lemons springing from the branches! Yes, 43 lemons!

Why now?
Why this year?
Who cares?

I am joyous and admiring of my lemon tree from every angle. I really don't need an agricultural reason to explain the harvest. The time is right, at last, for my lemon and I to rejoice! My dreams are coming true – and that's the thing with dreams isn't it? There's never a defined date as with achieving an ambitious goal.

A dream is a mixture of desire, vision, hope, expectancy, and a gift to yourself. And when a dream comes true, turns into reality, there is no surprise if you have held it in your heart, just gratitude that it has happened.

About The Author

Mary Rose Selman has spent the last 26 years as an Independent Sales Director with the legendary American Skin Care Company Mary Kay Cosmetics.

As a UK Top Five ranked Independent Senior Sales Director with Mary Kay, she has spent the last 26 years recruiting and training a large number of independent sales consultants, and mentoring Independent Sales Directors in direct selling, team-building, customer service, and product knowledge, in the UK, Switzerland, Eire and Germany.

Born and raised in Yorkshire, Mary Rose graduated American High School near Boston Massachusetts, before continuing her further education in Modern Dance at the Laban Studio in Surrey, then qualifying as a teacher in 1974. Having married Jeremy in 1975, Mary Rose worked as a Primary School teacher in Leicestershire.

While taking time out to raise their two children, she wrote two internationally best-selling education books for teachers, and was commissioned to write further books on English Language for parents of primary aged children. She eventually became a Deputy Head Teacher in Gloucestershire before changing careers and joining Mary Kay Cosmetics in 1993.

Here she found her 'happy place' initially working with world class Mary Kay cosmetics products, and then focussing on helping women to achieve being the best they can be, through creating harmony around core values of faith, family and career.

Realising that all her skills were transferable to all types of business, Mary Rose created her consultancy business 'Sell the Difference' which provides training and mentoring for individuals and small businesses in sales performance, presentation skills, personality profiling and other core business needs. She is a Certified DiSC® Trainer.

A founding member of the South Lakes/Lancashire group 'Women Interested in Networking Knowledge' (WINK), Mary Rose is in increasing demand as a public speaker. From 2014, she has been a student mentor on the Lancaster University Career Mentoring Programme, and has given workshops on image and confidence both at the University and the local Further Education College.

A keen walker and gardener, Mary Rose divides her time between living in Lancashire and cherishing an olive grove in Umbria, Italy.

Other Publications by the Author

Mary Rose Selman and Mary Baird (1986) *Primary Teacher's Handbook*, A guide to supply teaching, Oliver and Boyd, Edinburgh.

Mary Rose Selman (1989) *Infant Teacher's Handbook*, Oliver and Boyd, Edinburgh.

Mary Rose Selman (1990) *Getting Ahead in English*, Shared learning activities, Longman, Harlow.

Mary Rose Selman and Mary Baird (1991) *Primary Teacher's Handbook K-7*, Units of work in popular themes for 5-12 year olds, Longman Cheshire, Melbourne.

Mary Rose Selman and Mary Baird (1992) *The Practical Teacher's Handbook Part 1*, Whole language themes for 5-12 year olds, Longman Cheshire, Melbourne.

Mary Rose Selman and Mary Baird (1992) *The Practical Teacher's Handbook Part 2*, Whole language themes for 5-12 year olds, Longman Cheshire, Melbourne.

Acknowledgements

Rather like the tip of the iceberg, the finished book belies all the efforts it takes to produce. I am grateful and wish to acknowledge so many people who have directly or indirectly added to *Under the Sales Umbrella*.

My loyal customers who taught me about how to make sales all about customer service. My friends and colleagues in Mary Kay Cosmetics around the world for providing a complete support structure so necessary in any business, and exceptional in our 'Pink' world. I salute you!

Special thanks go to my friends who have read, re-read, commented, advised and encouraged: Yvonne Williams, Amanda Green, Helyn Connerr, and last but by no means least, Cathy Ranford, whose sales example I have followed admiringly for 25 years!

A very special thank you to Katie and Lou, my talented, gifted friends, for interpreting ideas and creating images with wit and style!

Thank you to Katie Edwards for the cover design.

Thank you to Lou Simmonds for the illustrations.

Under the Sales Umbrella would never have been more than an idea without my husband Jeremy. He has encouraged, cajoled, typed, edited, insisted and advised. He has the patience of a Saint, but never let me lose sight of the reason: to write it all down! You always said there was another book to write and here it is, with my love and thanks.

Notes